Growing Together in Christ

by

Gene Gronholz and Mark Zarling

MARRIAGE

NORTHWESTERN PUBLISHING HOUSE
Milwaukee, Wisconsin

Library of Congress Card 96-71666
Northwestern Publishing House
1250 N. 113th St., Milwaukee, WI 53226-3284
© 1996 by Northwestern Publishing House.
Published 1996
Printed in the United States of America
ISBN 0-8100-0698-7

Contents

Introduction

Loving, nurturing, mutually satisfying marriages don't happen by chance. Successful marriages require a clear perception of God's design and plan for marriage. In addition, couples can benefit from an understanding of proven principles that can help them form loving relationships and grow in those relationships.

God, who is the designer and creator of marriage, desires that you enjoy all the joy, satisfaction, and blessings of a Christ-centered marriage. Are you and your spouse experiencing all that God intended your marriage to be? Or, are you and your spouse feeling frustrated in your relationship?

This book can help those about to be married and those who have been married for many years. If your marriage is reaching the crisis stage, this book is for you too. The ideas and principles discussed in it can give a lift to any marriage.

As you begin to put the ideas and principles in this book into action, don't expect changes to happen overnight. If you have problems in your relationship, they did not develop overnight, and they will not go away overnight. Your relationship requires your undivided attention and commitment to change. If you and your spouse are committed to change, make God an integral part in the changes you want to implement. God will bless your efforts because God wants your marriage to be happy.

May this book be a blessing to all who read it. May it ultimately glorify God's name and further his kingdom.

CHAPTER 1:

A View of Marriage:
from the Garden of Eden
to the Present

In one of his wars, Cyrus of Persia took captive an Armenian princess. He condemned her to death. When her husband heard of her fate, he came into the camp of his conqueror and offered his life in place of his wife. Cyrus was so touched with the devotion of the prince that he pardoned them both.

Officers and soldiers of Cyrus marveled at the touching generosity of their great leader. The princess stood near them, her eyes filled with tears. One of the officers turned to her and asked, "What do you think of Cyrus?"

"I was not thinking of Cyrus," she answered.

"Of whom, then were you thinking?" he asked.

Looking up into the face of her husband, her eyes luminous with love, she answered, "I was thinking of the one who would willingly have died for me."[1]

The story poses some questions for husbands. What do husbands think of the prince's willingness to give his life for his wife? Was he acting irrationally? Or was he showing unselfish devotion, love, and commitment to her? How many husbands in a similar situation would be willing to do the same for their wives?

But there are questions for wives too. What thoughts do wives have about the prince? Would they respond: I can't imagine my husband ever doing that for me? What made this man love his wife so deeply? What did she do to be so loved? What message was in her eyes as she turned to him?

Marriage partners whose feelings are tangled and confused would probably say something like, "It's a daily struggle to show love." Husbands who struggle in their marriages would probably respond, "The way I'm feeling about my wife right now, I don't think so." Wives who are caught in troubled marriages might say, "I don't think I've ever felt that kind of devotion. I sure do envy the princess."

But, God intended marriage to be a blessing to husbands and wives. If God intended marriage to be a blessing, then why don't more marriages give blessings? Why are so many marriages becoming stagnant? Why do spouses continue drifting farther and farther apart instead of drawing closer together? Why are some husbands and wives inflicting such pain on each other and on their children?

Some problems for marriage: the human heart

What answers can we find for all the discontent and pain of broken marriages and broken homes? First, we can look into the human heart. Each separate human heart comes with its own set of weaknesses and imperfections. As Christians we know those human weaknesses are symptoms of our sinful nature. King David knew it was true. He wrote, "Surely I was sinful at birth, sinful from the time my mother conceived me" (Psalm 51:5). What an indictment! What a confession!

Each separate human heart comes

with its own set of weaknesses and imperfections.

We can learn a couple things from David's words. He was like all humans. We all enter this world plagued by the same problem. Because of our sinful nature, each life will show evidence of it in the actions and relationships of everyday living. Hatred, jealousy, fits of rage, selfishness, envy, drunkenness, sexual immorality all come from our sinful nature. (Read Galatians 5:19-26.) How many of these problems influence marriage? Don't they all have the potential of destroying love and frustrating happiness? Sadly, we all carry the seeds of our own unhappiness into the relationship from which we expect the greatest joy.

Sadly, we all carry the seeds of our own unhappiness into the relationship from which we expect the greatest joy.

But there is one more thing we can learn from David. He confesses that he is the sinner. He did not look at someone else and find all the mistakes in that other person. Instead he was brutally honest about himself. Of course, he lived with others who were equally sinful, but he looked at himself and discovered that he was one that could bring misery and unhappiness on himself and others. Remember. He did! He took another man's wife and then ordered her husband murdered. Then he covered up his actions. We don't go to the extremes of David's actions, but lust, envy, lies, and guilt lurk within each human heart as they did in David's. But David teaches us to look at ourselves first. When we blame someone else and look at the mistakes and failures of our spouse first, we easily dismiss our own contribution to our marital unhappiness.

Some problems for marriage: our anti-marriage world

Are there other reasons for troubled marriages? Of course. Consider the attitude toward marriage in our world today. To witness firsthand a vivid portrait of modern America's view of marriage, one needs only to turn on the television set. There in living color on virtually any network, the viewer can observe a blatant disregard of the sanctity of marriage. The pleasure of sex overpowers any idea of commitment. Happy marriages don't often exist on network prime time. Some who speak up for the sanctity of marriage on talk shows meet boos and ridicule. In addition, what one sees in many magazines and what one hears in the lyrics of much of today's music shows the continuing attack on marriage as we approach the twenty-first century.

In contemporary America, more and more signs point to a lack of commitment regarding marriage. There is also an attitude: I gotta be me; I gotta do my own thing. The K-Mart or Wal-Mart syndrome is replacing "till death us do part." One thing both these retail giants pride themselves on is the promise that if their customers aren't satisfied with their purchase, they can bring it back and get one of comparable value, or they can get a complete refund. How many couples today walk down the aisle with the attitude: we'll give it a try, but if it doesn't work out we can always take it back?

The flip side is the growing tendency to experiment with marriage without marrying. When asked why they have a live-in boyfriend or girlfriend, they respond, "Right now our love is so strong, we don't need a marriage license, marriage certificate, or ring. It's better this way because if our feelings change toward each other, we are free to leave. We don't feel tied down. It's less of a hassle." How can we as a people, a society, expect to preserve and protect relationships between men and women when God's unique, sacred plan for marriage is no longer seen as relevant?

Some problems for marriage: Satan

Another factor behind all the discontent and pain in so many marriages is the work of the father of lies, Satan himself. Satan hates God; he hates marriage, which God established for his creatures, Adam and Eve. Already in the Garden of Eden, Satan attacked God's beautiful and perfect plan for marriage with a barrage of distortions and lies. As we know from reading Genesis chapter 3, Adam and Eve succumbed to his lies. From that time on, marriage changed. Sins of inconsideration, blame, accusation, selfishness, and a host of others invaded and tainted what was good.

From the Garden of Eden to the present, Satan unrelentingly demonstrates his opposition to God by waging all-out war against marriage. Why? Because Satan knows that God wanted marriage to be the keystone of society and the church. Family life revolves around the relationship between husband and wife. Children learn about life and God through their relationship with their parents. Christian parents take Solomon's advice seriously: "Train a child in the way he should go, and when he is old he will not turn from it" (Proverbs 22:6). What better way for Satan to attack God and his believers than to attack the holy estate of marriage—that which God holds in such high esteem and which is the very foundation of the home, church, state, nation, and world.

From the Garden of Eden to the present,
Satan unrelentingly demonstrates his opposition to God
by waging all-out war against marriage.

Over the course of time, Satan accomplishes his goal of discrediting and mocking God by weaving distortions and lies regarding marriage into the very fabric of man's mind and society. Satan prompts the hearts of men and women to move away from, ignore, and dishonor God's marriage plan. As attitudes about the sanctity of marriage change, marriage becomes less honored. As marriage becomes less honored, broken homes, as a result of broken marriages, become a reality even in Christian lives and homes.

Over the course of time,
Satan accomplishes his goal of discrediting and mocking God
by weaving distortions and lies regarding marriage
into the very fabric of man's mind and society.

Some problems for marriage: an age-old problem

As one studies history, one would be led to the realization that no age is better than the ones that preceded it. In the book of Malachi 2:13-16, God rebuked the Old Testament Israelites regarding marriage with these words:

> Another thing you do: You flood the LORD's altar with tears. You weep and wail because he no longer pays attention to your offerings or accepts them with pleasure from your hands. You ask, "Why?" It is because the LORD is acting as the witness between you and the wife of your youth, because you have broken faith with her, though she is your partner, the wife of your marriage covenant. Has not the LORD made them one? In flesh and spirit they are his. And why one? Because he was seeking godly offspring. So guard yourself in your spirit, and do not break faith with the wife of your youth. "I hate divorce," says the LORD God of Israel, "and I hate a man's covering himself with violence as well as with his garment," says the LORD Almighty. So guard yourself in your spirit, and do not break faith.

If Luther were alive today and could see how contemporary America views marriage, he would, no doubt, be led to the same conclusion he reached in his own day. Luther made a clear distinction between how the world and the believers see marriage when he wrote:

> The world says of marriage, A short joy and a long displeasure. But let it say whatever it please. Whatever God has created and wants is bound to be a mockery to it. What kind of pleasure and joy the world finds outside marriage, I think it will best become aware of in its conscience. To be married and to understand married life are two very different matters. He who is married but does not understand married life can never live in it without displeasure, trouble, and misery. He must complain and slander, as the heathen and unreasoning, blind people do. But he who understands it finds in it delight, love, and joy without ceasing, as Solomon says: "Whoso findeth a wife findeth a good thing" (Proverbs 18:22). These are the people who understand, who firmly believe that God has instituted marriage and joined man and woman together.[2]

Christian husbands and wives need to be on guard. They need to remain vigilant and alert to Satan's attacks on their thoughts and feelings regarding their marriage vows. In the darkest hours of confusion, hurt, and disappointment, Satan will come with all kinds of reasons to justify thoughts such as, "This marriage is not going to work, we just are not meant for each other."

Overcoming the problems

So how can people overcome these problems and build better marriages? That's what this book is all about. Building and maintaining a marriage and a home requires work, *joint work*, and sometimes difficult work. If you are reading this book alone, I suggest that you read it together with your spouse and talk about it. Some exercises to help you will be found at the end of each chapter. I would also ask that you take your marriage to the Lord in prayer. Pray for his blessing on you, your spouse, and your children. Ask for the fruits of the Spirit: love, joy, peace, patience, kindness, goodness, faithfulness, gentleness, and self-control. Then turn to God's Word because God will give you these blessings through the Word. If you don't use his Word, he does not have access to your heart and cannot work to give you what you ask. He has promised to work through the Word.

> *Building and maintaining a marriage and a home requires work,* joint work, *and sometimes difficult work.*

Where shall you start? Start at the beginning. When God brought Adam and Eve together, he had some definite ideas about what marriage should be. Anyone who has ever built a house knows that without a plan the excavator, masons, carpenters, electricians, and plumbers would experience disharmony and confusion. Someone, an architect, needs to develop a plan—one that works. Let's look at God's plan for marriage. Husbands need to know what marriage is and what married life can and should be. Wives need the same knowledge. If you don't know God's plan, no wonder you are experiencing, in the words of Luther, "displeasure, trouble, and misery."

Start at your own beginning as husband or wife. Whether your marriage started in a church or not, you stood before God who sees all we do and say. You started a family when you pledged to be faithful to your spouse. At that moment, you undoubtedly believed that your promise was more than just words. It was a commitment to yourself, to your spouse and, whether you realized it or not, also to God. Your marriage remains a commitment. All the hopes you had at your beginning can be recovered from the wreckage of neglect and confusion.

To those who are thinking this marriage is over or is never going to make it, you are encouraged to read the next chapter and come to better understand what a miracle God performed when he brought Adam and Eve together and established marriage and family.

May God equip you with "spiritual eyes" to see and understand his miracle of marriage.

EXERCISES

The following questions are exercises connected to the miracle of marriage. They are designed to do much more than flatten a stomach or tighten a thigh. God wants to create a new and loving you through his Son Jesus. Try these exercises, and be patient. We don't expect an exercise program to change our bodies in just three weeks. We shouldn't expect that our marriages will change overnight either.

1. Choose a television program you and your spouse either have watched or plan to watch. Write down what the program said about marriage and the relationships between men and women. Do those attitudes help marriages? Tell why or why not.

2. Discuss your notes on the television program with your spouse. This may be difficult at first, but ask, "Do you think . . ." and then listen.

3. List what you hoped your marriage would be on the day you were married. Ask your spouse to do the same thing. Compare your lists.

4. Go to church together as a couple or as a family if you have children.

CHAPTER 2:

The Miracle of Marriage

Do you believe in miracles? I'm not talking about good luck, fate, or happy coincidence. Most people live their lives hoping for some kind of miracle. Some hope for the "miracle" of winning the lottery. Others long for the "miracle" of instant popularity and the attention it seems to bring. Still others want some "miracle" to come and straighten out all the problems in this world or in their own lives.

Such hopes for a "miracle" are not at all realistic. But that's what miracles are. A miracle may appear to be simply chance. It is an event that takes place even against laws of nature and against common sense or experience. Do you believe in that kind of miracle? I suppose we all do because we have heard of such miracles. People have been healed in spite of the failure of medical knowledge and expertise. Healing has occurred, and the doctors have absolutely no explanation except that it happened. Others have been saved from terrible and hopeless circumstances by a seemingly freakish occurrence.

As Christians, we do believe in miracles. After all, Scripture over and over again records the mighty miracles of the Lord Jesus. He quieted furious storms. He healed crippled limbs. He fed ravenous crowds. Miracles are accepted as fact in the biblical record. We believe the Lord did perform miracles long ago for many who needed his intervention.

Going to the One who works miracles

So do you believe in miracles? That question becomes more difficult to answer when it becomes personal. Do you believe in miracles in your own life? Do you honestly believe that our loving Savior can intervene and make a difference in your life, in your home, in your marriage? You might answer, "I'd have to believe in a miracle to salvage this marriage. It's beyond hope." Well, miracles do occur. Marriage itself is a miracle of God. He makes two separate, independent people one. God said, "For this reason a man will leave his father and mother and be united to his wife, and they will become one flesh" (Genesis 2:24). The miracle can evaporate like dew in the heat of day-to-day life. Yet God can perform the miracle of healing painful and destroyed marriages too.

Do you honestly believe that our loving Savior
can intervene and make a difference in your life,
in your home, in your marriage?

Perhaps you picked up this little book precisely for that reason. Your marriage is in crisis. At least, you recognize that you need help. Scripture tells us that we need a miracle in order to change our attitudes and behavior. We simply do not have the power to "pull ourselves up by the bootstraps." No, we are helpless by ourselves to solve any problem that has its root in sin. A wise missionary once said, "I know that nothing good lives in me, that is, in my sinful nature. For I have the desire to do what is good, but I cannot carry it out. For what I do is not the good I want to do; no, the evil I do not want to do—this I keep on doing" (Romans 7:18,19). We need miracles to change our behavior. Where can we go?

Sometimes we go to the wrong places for help. If your expensive Swiss watch suddenly stopped, would you take it to your neighbor across the street to fix it? While sipping a cup of coffee, would you spread it out on the kitchen table and listen to advice on how to fix it? Would you take it off at a bar and give it to your drinking buddy to fix after he has had two or three drinks? Would you go downstairs to your workbench and take out your hammer and pliers and go at it? Why do we treat our marriages as if they are cheaper than some watch? The source of miracles is the Master Craftsman, the Creator and Savior of all. We have the comfort and hope that this Craftsman can fix anything. No matter how impossible the situation might seem right now, remember what Jesus once said, "With man this is impossible, but with God all things are possible" (Matthew 19:26).

Sometimes we go to the wrong places for help.

So if it is going to take a miracle to fix your marriage, then go to the one who works miracles. Christ can do miracles. His Easter resurrection proves it. He has the power not only over life and death but over every part of our lives. I believe that marriage, as God truly intends it to be, is nothing short of a miracle. Christ alone can build this miracle, fix it, and sustain it. Christ and his Word make a marriage a Christian marriage.

Now of course, God blesses even the marriages of those who do not believe in Jesus. Purely out of grace and for the good of society, God blesses the marriages of believers and unbelievers. Jesus said, "He [God] causes his sun to rise on the evil and the good, and sends rain on the righteous and the unrighteous" (Matthew 5:45). But the Lord is especially interested in the spiritual and physical welfare of those who trust in him. Believers in Jesus understand the special miracle he works in a marriage where the Savior is at the center. But before we look at fixing the problems of marriage, I want to review the miracle of a Christian marriage.

Marriage is a miracle that Christ created

More and more people are trying to redefine marriage through prenuptial agreements, marriage contacts, homosexual marriages, and on and on. Don't expect the world to teach us about the miracle of marriage. It cannot. It will not. Contrary to modern anthropologists, marriage is not some product of an evolutionary process. Over a period of time, humans did not conveniently come to some understanding over copulation or how to cooperate in chores and child rearing. Marriage is not mating in the same way that birds and creatures mate to ensure another generation of similar creatures. Marriage is much more. It is a divine arrangement that the Lord devised from the beginning for the good of his children. Since God joined a man and woman together in marriage, we had best look to him for directions.

> *Since God joined a man and woman together in marriage, we had best look to him for directions.*

If we go back to the beginning through the record God himself gave to us, we can review God's plan for this institution called marriage. The Scriptures are God's record of events he has carefully preserved for our benefit. The words of Genesis are words God gave to Moses by inspiration. They are not words flowing from man's imagination or from his deep desire to create the perfect world.

Genesis tells us that God created a perfect man and placed him in the Garden of Eden. "God saw all that he had made, and it was very good" (Genesis 1:31). This man was not a self-centered "coach potato." The first husband was not an arrogant "macho" man. Nor was he a brute only slightly smarter than an ape. He was perfect and holy, created in the image of God. Yet God also said, "It is not good for the man to be alone. I will make a helper suitable for him" (Genesis 2:18). So God had Adam name all the creatures and animals. Why? God opened Adam's eyes to see a simple fact. No matter how perfect he was, he was not complete. Every animal had a partner, but Adam was unique and alone. Adam had been created in the image of God. He had a soul; he was intelligent; he was accountable to his Creator and at one with God's will. No other creature had been made with such unique blessings and identity. Adam was truly different and alone. When Adam named the animals, he began to seek the blessing that the Lord in love and grace had planned. When Adam understood his needs, then God created a helper suitable for him.

A "helper suitable" does not mean a rival or a competitor. God intended to create someone appropriate, someone to supply what the man lacked. In other words, God intended Eve to be a complement to Adam. He created them both so that there were differences between a man and a woman. Their differences were more than just physical. God intended that those differences be cherished and nurtured. When the differences are joined together, there is a completeness, a union that did not exist before.

Men and women are different in more ways than just the obvious physical differences. We will examine some of these basic physiological differences in a later chapter. For right now, remember that God made humans male and female. We dare not use the differences between men and women to start arguments. The differences do not mean that one sex is better than the other. Pointing fingers or heaping shame and guilt upon one another because of our differences is not God's intent. We dare not try to change the differences either: society's efforts toward androgyny are against God's plan of creation. In the marriage relationship, we don't need to try to make our spouse think more like we think. We need someone to think differently than we do, to help us see another perspective, to find a completeness and union through our differences.

In marriage especially, it is essential to learn to accept each other; more than that, to cherish each other for what God has made us. Think of that divine surgery in the Garden of Eden. Why did God take a rib from Adam to form Eve? The Lord could have created the woman in the exact same manner as he created man. God could have taken dust, formed a female, and breathed into her the breath of life. But he did not. He formed the woman from the man. Adam understood that sermon. Eve was Adam's suitable other, made from the same flesh but different. He said, "This is now bone of my bones and flesh of my flesh; she shall be called 'woman' for she was taken out of man" (Genesis 2:23). A Christian husband views his wife as a special creation of God, whom God brought to him. Although there are two individuals with unique abilities, temperaments, likes and dislikes, God seeks to create a new identity. He seeks to create a union and a new oneness. This identity is shared in the union. I am not fully myself without my spouse. Nor is she fully herself without me.

The gift of our sexuality reflects this miracle of two becoming one. God's gift of sex is not to be some instinctive mating ritual. Sex with another is an intimate giving to another. God intended a man and a woman to share even their bodies as an expression of commitment to each other in a lifelong union. The physical union is to be an intimate expression of the union that exists between a husband and a wife on all levels of their lives—emotional, mental, spiritual. Apart from the miracle of marriage, sexual intimacy is always and only a selfish expression of pleasure, power, or manipulation. But as God intends it, sexual intercourse becomes an act of loving and sharing, not lusting and taking.

Apart from the miracle of marriage,
sexual intimacy is always and only a selfish expression
of pleasure, power, or manipulation.

Do we think this is all a pious fairy tale? Is it unrealistic? The Pharisees at Christ's time thought so. They came to Jesus and tried to trick him. They didn't think very highly of marriage and favored their own version of "no-fault divorce." There is nothing new under the sun; marriage was attacked then as it is now. But Jesus reminded them that marriage is a miracle of God's creation. Jesus quoted the creation account and went back to God's plan to explain the basics of marriage. Christ said, "Haven't you read . . . that at the beginning the Creator 'made them male and female,' and said, 'For this reason a man will leave his father and mother and be united to his wife, and the two will become one flesh'? So they are no longer two, but one. Therefore what God has joined together, let man not separate" (Matthew 19:4-6).

Marv and Lois had celebrated their golden wedding anniversary. The whole family came home for the celebration. But two weeks later, Marv was dead. The man with whom Lois had shared half a century had been called to heaven. How hard it was to cope! She imagined she could still hear his voice each morning. He had regularly made coffee in the kitchen. Now life didn't seem right any more. After years and years together, she was alone. And part of her was gone. Ask any widow or widower what it is like to adjust after losing a lifelong spouse, and they will almost always say, "Part of me is gone." Marriage is a miraculous union in which two people truly do grow together and become one.

God's miracle spoiled

Unfortunately, God's perfect plan for the happiness of Adam and Eve—the first marriage—was quickly ruined. Genesis relates the rebellion of our first parents in chapter 3. Listening to the father of lies, Adam and Eve ate of the forbidden fruit, disobeying the command of their heavenly Father. Sin is selfishness. Eve was selfish in wanting to eat of the fruit, disregarding her Creator's will. Adam was selfish in eating from his wife's hand, knowingly going against the command that God had personally given him before Eve was created. Such selfishness is at the root of every transgression of the First Commandment. "I don't care what God wants. I want to do it my way." That rebellion devastated creation. After it, more than weeds began to grow in the garden. Adam and Eve discovered a new array of feelings: fear, guilt, worry, and distrust. Death entered creation. Both of them attempted the impossible: hiding from God. Adam blamed God. Eve blamed the serpent.

Such sinful ideas are quick to enter the marriage. Satan still tricks us with his lies. He quickly has us excusing our own sins and weaknesses and pointing the finger of blame at someone else. "If only she would quit nagging me all the time." "If only he would be more understanding and considerate." Marriage, because of sin, often becomes the battleground for proving who's right. How quickly we forget the need to confess that "there is no one righteous, not even one; . . . there is no one who does good, not even one. . . . There is no difference, for all have sinned and fall short of the glory of God" (Romans 3:10,12,22,23).

Satan still tricks us with his lies.
He quickly has us excusing our own sins and weaknesses
and pointing the finger of blame at someone else.

Sin has spoiled God's beautiful miracle. Turmoil replaces peace in our hearts and homes. No longer are two people eager to make a lasting and lifelong commitment. No longer are two quick to sacrifice to make one. It does take a miracle to make a marriage work when two sinful humans are involved—so powerful and self-centered are our egos. How we need Jesus. By his power working through his Word, he can peel away our pride and sin! How we need Jesus to use his Word to expose our personal sins and wrongs. Making a marriage work is not a matter of changing the other person. It starts with one heart and soul—yours. And only the Lord Jesus can change you through his Word.

Marriage still takes a miracle that only Christ can create

When is the last time you took inventory of your marriage? What do you think the problems are? What is the root of the disagreements and tensions? Would love, peace, patience, kindness, faithfulness, gentleness, and self-control help your marriage? How much does hatred, discord, jealousy, fits of rage, and ambition distort the relationship between husband and wife? Have things deteriorated so badly that your marriage is now viewed as a burden and not a blessing, a curse rather than a comfort?

How can you help cultivate the positive attitudes while weeding out the negative ones? That's a challenge for any married couple. When troubles and disagreements strain the relationship, it is especially challenging. Clearing the marriage of its weeds requires an internal change for each partner. The first place to begin working for change is not in your partner, however. You do have an influence on your partner, but you cannot change your spouse unless you are ready to change yourself. Even then perhaps the best you can do is change yourself and hope that as you change, you can help your spouse to change too.

Clearing the marriage of its weeds
requires an internal change for each partner.

A change from discord, jealousy, and rage to peace, faithfulness, and gentleness is a miracle. Jesus wants to give you such a miracle, and he can. How? Jesus is in the business of changing hearts. He changed our hearts from sin and unbelief to faith and love. That was a miracle we could not have done ourselves. He chose us and worked this great change within us. Because Jesus has changed our hearts, we are capable of peace, faithfulness, and gentleness. Our sinful nature is still just as capable of discord, jealousy, and rage. Inside we have a war going on every day between the weeds of sin and the green pastures of God's love and grace.

Not only did Jesus awaken faith in your heart, but he performs miracles every day whenever we are peace loving, faithful, and gentle instead of jealous, angry, and argumentative. Are you still wondering how? Jesus changed us through his words of love and forgiveness, the gospel. He has promised to continue to work within us through the same gospel. When we hear and read the gospel or when we receive the assurance of forgiveness in the Lord's Supper, the Holy Spirit works to strengthen us so we can cultivate the virtues of Christian living.

Don't think this has nothing to do with marriage. It has everything to do with marriage. A commitment to marriage is first and foremost a commitment to the Lord God and his way of doing things. A commitment to his holy Word works, for he promises: "It [my word] will not return to me empty, but will accomplish what I desire and achieve the purpose for which I sent it" (Isaiah 55:11). The Holy Spirit of God uses the gospel to create a relationship with Jesus as Savior. Hearts are changed by God's grace. We know forgiveness because Jesus has changed us. We know peace with God because of the miracle of faith. Once we know and love Jesus, our hearts are eager to live to the glory of the One who loved us first. Christian marriage is but one way to reflect our love and thanks to the Lord Jesus.

God wants you to see your spouse as a soul, one for whom Christ died. Can you look into your wife's or husband's eyes and say, "I want to see you in heaven"? The answer to that question will determine the attitude with which you read this book. And if the answer is yes, then you can begin to find shelter from all the attacks on your marriage. Satan will throw grenades of guilt and bombs of blame into your relationship. Perhaps he has been doing that for some time already. If you don't do something, the problems will demolish your relationship with Jesus, the only Savior, and wreck your relationship with your spouse. The dangerous consequence will become quickly evident: "I don't care what Jesus says. I want a divorce." But a commitment to the Word of Jesus Christ will be blessed by the Holy Spirit with a renewed commitment to Jesus and to each other. God does not lie. Jesus plainly says, "If you remain in me and my words remain in you, ask whatever you wish, and it will be given you. This is to my Father's glory, that you bear much fruit, showing yourselves to be my disciples" (John 15:7,8). Do you ask for a loving and forgiving heart? Do you ask for his help? He promises it to us as a miracle of the gospel.

Jesus says marriage is good,
a blessing he wants you to experience to the fullest.
Don't give up; give your marriage to the Lord Jesus.

Mary came into the pastor's office and sat down wearily. "Things are pretty bad at home. He moved out again. Every time we try to talk, we just end up fighting and yelling at each other. I don't think I love him anymore. I don't know if we should even try again. What's the use? Do you think you could do anything?"

"I'll be glad to meet with you," the pastor replies. "But let me ask you something. When was the last time we talked?"

Mary looked a bit uncomfortable as she replied, "Well, Pastor, I haven't been coming to church lately."

"I know. I haven't seen either you or your husband at church for some time. Apart from the gospel, faith grows weak and withers. How can we expect to have an attitude of forgiving love that flows from the cross of Jesus if we haven't taken time to hear and learn of that love?"

"I know, Pastor, but I just don't feel up to attending church."

"I can understand that because I know you're hurting. But I'm not a fix-it man. I can't fix your problems and neither can you, all by yourself. I will try to take you back into God's Word, so you learn to confess your wrongs to God and to each other. I want to teach you God's plan for your happiness and the power source of Christ's forgiving love that makes that plan possible. I am also going to ask you to agree to come to the Lord's house, not just once in a while, but every week. Things are critical between you and your husband. The problems cannot be resolved until things are right with you and the Lord Jesus. Come and hear his good news: "Take heart . . . your sins are forgiven" (Matthew 9:2). If you begin to hear God's promises regularly, then with God's help we can work at the problems. But if you don't want to go that route, I'm not going to be able to help you."

Is it worth the effort? Your Savior says yes. Marriage is a miracle that God still calls good. He wants you to have the confidence that Jesus can cover all past wrongs, no matter how serious, with his blood. Jesus can soothe the souls and heal the hearts. Jesus says marriage is good, a blessing he wants you to experience to the fullest. Don't give up; give your marriage to the Lord Jesus. Pray that he may use the practical advice in the remainder of this little book to be a blessing to you as you pray for a stronger and happier marriage. It will take a miracle, but Jesus is in the miracle business.

EXERCISES

1. Write a prayer based on the Third Petition ("Your will be done on earth as in heaven") and apply it to your marriage. What is God's will for your marriage? What do you want Jesus to give to you? What do you want Jesus to give to your spouse? How do you want Jesus to change you?

2. Learn to cherish the unique differences that you and your spouse have. List four or five special gifts that make your husband or wife unique and different from any other.

3. Read Song of Songs together. Paraphrase parts of it to write love poems to each other.

4. Go to church together and discuss what God said to you in his Word.

CHAPTER 3:

The Unique Differences between Men and Women

It has become clearer, while working with married couples, that many marriage difficulties result from the fact that men and women really don't understand how different they are from each other. Marriage partners will find it difficult to meaningfully communicate love and nurturing or meet each other's physical, emotional, and sexual needs until they understand the unique differences between men and women.

Listen to Betty's story:

Betty, in her early 30s and a mother of two girls, struggled to find the words to describe the pain that was written all over her face.

- "I don't think my husband, Dan, loves me anymore."

- "He doesn't talk to me. When I talk to him he doesn't listen."

- "When he comes home from work, he sits down and eats supper. Then, for the rest of the night, he reads the newspaper and watches television."

- "He doesn't help me with the girls."

- "I feel all I'm good for is to cook, wash clothes, clean the house, and wait on him."

- "He bowls twice a week, goes to football and basketball games with his friends, but he never asks me if I would like to go along.

I can't remember the last time he took me out for dinner and a movie."

- "I'm worried he might be seeing another woman. When I think about it, it terrifies me!"

- "I feel so alone, so rejected, so unloved and unappreciated."

- "We don't pray together; we don't attend church regularly."

- The tears came freely as she shared how depressed and lonely she felt. "I can't stand the coldness anymore. I'm seriously thinking about leaving Dan."

Betty described how she felt about her relationship with Dan. "I feel so alone, so rejected, so unloved." What Betty was describing is a feeling of isolation. Betty felt Dan was excluding her from his life. As a result of that isolation, Betty felt a lack of closeness, a lack of intimacy. How does it happen that love and closeness can turn to isolation?

Listen to Dan's side of the story:

In a separate interview with Dan, he shared,

- "I don't know Betty anymore."

- "She is constantly criticizing me for things I didn't get done around the house."

- "She doesn't have time for me. She devotes all her time to the girls."

- "I wonder at times what I'm good for."

- "I work hard, but I don't think I get much respect from Betty. We can't say anything to each other without yelling at one another; that's why I find things to do on my own."

- "Our sex life is practically nonexistent."

- "There has to be more to life than this! It's even hard for me to pray about our problems."

Dan felt excluded from Betty's life as well. He described it in words such as, "I don't know Betty anymore. . . . She doesn't have time for me. . . . Our sex life is practically nonexistent."

Betty and Dan shared the same bed, ate at the same table, raised the same children; they occupied the same house, but both felt alone. Betty and Dan talked about the mortgage and car payments, the girls' dentist appointments, and where they would like to spend Christmas, but they weren't really communicating. They did occasionally go to church together, they both attended parent-teacher meetings, they sat together at school activities, but they really didn't share life with each other. Neither Betty nor Dan understood what the other needed. As husband and wife, they were different. Their differences isolated them by becoming barriers to their love and understanding. They could not find a way for their differences to complement one another because they didn't know the differences.

Our society has focused our attention almost exclusively on the equality of the sexes. Unfortunately, that emphasis overlooks the differences and robs us of an important aspect of healthy relationships between men and women—recognizing and valuing the important differences between the sexes. Even in relationships where typical gender roles are reversed, different male and female styles predominate.

Some differences between men and women

So, let's explore the differences between men and women that are so vital to healthy marriage relationships. Remember that a full exploration of the differences requires a complete book. For our purposes in this chapter, we will summarize the significant differences and refer to some of the psychological research on this topic. The overview will give you a place to begin and provide an elementary understanding of the differences. With this simple knowledge, hopefully you can begin to explore those differences and develop a better relationship with your spouse.

Why are males and females so different? The answer for Christians is simple: God made them different. He has different roles for them. Therefore in his wisdom he equipped them with the emotional, physical, sexual, and intuitive tools necessary to fulfill their roles. The contemporary world has lost focus on the differences because technology has altered the way we find food, the way we defend our territory and confront threats, and even the way we rear children. Yet the differences remain.

Right brain vs. left brain

The differences between men and women show up already in childhood. As children, we all came to the realization that boys and girls are different in the way they play, the clothes they wear, the toys they prefer and, in some situations, the sports they play. What is evident to everyone observing children is clear even earlier. Dr. Frank Duffy of Boston Children's Hospital recorded brain activity of boys and girls before they were born. His research discovered that boys' and girls' brains function on different wavelengths.

How did that happen? Additional research discovered that an event takes place sometime between the 18th and 26th week of pregnancy that makes the development of boys different from that of girls. During that period boys receive a chemical bath of testosterone and other sex-related hormones. When those chemicals hit the boys' systems, the right side of the brain recedes slightly. The chemical bath also destroys some of the tissue connecting the right and left sides of the brain.

Remember that the human brain is divided into two halves, or hemispheres. The left side of the brain controls the logical, analytical, and factual functions of human activity. The right side harbors the center for emotions, communication, and relationship skills.

The left side of the brain controls the logical, analytical, and factual functions of human activity. The right side harbors the center for emotions, communication, and relationship skills.

What is the result of this testosterone bath for boys? Well, a boy starts life being more left-brain oriented. Girls come into the world more two-sided in their thinking. From the womb boys and girls already have a tendency toward different ways of thinking. Often we want to engage in some battle of the sexes and argue over which way is better. But one is not better than the other, just different. Instead of competing, we need to complement each other. We need each other. Men need the woman's perspective, and women need the man's perspective.

What do the differences mean for men in the real world? Because the left brain dominates for boys or men, they tend to be more logical and aggressive. Men utilize the left side of their brains for the majority of their waking hours. They enjoy conquering the obstacles of a long family vacation, storing dictionary definitions, and generally favor clinical, matter-of-fact thinking. Psychological literature confirms these observations.

Although girls and women are also logical and can fix things, men are usually more likely to buy *Popular Mechanics* or a how-to magazine in order to discover how to fix something around the house or the car in the garage. Men can memorize batting averages and box scores and will sit for hours watching sporting events and yelling at the officials. But left-brain orientation has some advantages too. The decision to start a major project and the self-discipline to carry it out come from this side of the brain. It seems that setting goals and working to achieve them are also a part of this orientation. But there are some disadvantages too. Left-brain orientation fails to understand relationships and feelings. At times people who are left-brained have difficulty communicating.

Women, on the other hand, have a right-brain orientation. Most of their days and nights are spent using the other side of the human brain. Because of that, most women can do fine detailed work, have flashes of imagination, and can enjoy an afternoon of art and fine music. They may not care about athletic events unless they personally know either one of the players or the wife of a player. They will buy *People* magazine and romance novels because, unlike men, they are more interested in relationships. While a man would store the dictionary definition of love, a woman would store the feelings associated with love.

By now, you may have begun to understand why communication between men and women is difficult. We need to continue our exploration of the differences. In the next sections of this chapter, the differences will be organized under four categories: Mental/Emotional, Physical, Sexual, and Intuitive.

Mental/Emotional differences

We all know men and women who defy the general differences I have outlined, but research does verify the general tendencies. We commonly categorize women as emotional. Unfortunately that has taken on some negative connotations. Yet what a positive thing it is. Women are more interested in people, feelings, and relationships than men. We commonly categorize men as practical and logical. We think of them as more competitive. These orientations also carry some negative connotations. Yet these attributes can also be positive.

Women are more interested in people, feelings, and relationships than men.

A woman's emotions are influenced by her role as childbearer. She is influenced by menstruation, lactation, and pregnancy. Men are not! Research also indicates that the hypothalamus, located at the base of the brain and called the "seat of the emotions," operates differently in women than it does in men. It is not surprising then that women are considered "emotional." When a woman becomes angry, she expresses it verbally. Men tend to express anger physically. These differences can create an explosive and destructive situation, which can lead to domestic violence. Yet because women are more interested in feelings and relationships, they will buy marriage books and have a strong desire to fix a broken relationship. Men do not demonstrate the same desire to build relationships with women or with others. Besides lacking the desire, they often lack the knowledge to build those relationships.

Dr. Cecil Osborne, in his book *The Art of Understanding Your Mate*, said, "One main characteristic which women possess is the innate tendency to be 'at one' with people and things, rather than viewing life from the outside. Women have the capacity to feel a sense of oneness with nature, people, and events more than most men."[1] "Though a man relates to people and situations, he usually doesn't allow his identity to become entwined with them. He somehow remains apart. That's why a woman, viewing her house as an extension of herself, can be hurt when it's criticized by others. A man may not realize it, but when he yells at the kids for something they did, his words affect [their mother] deeply as well."[2]

Gary Smalley, in *The Joy of Committed Love,* illustrates the differences in the way women adjust to change: "Women often need more time to adjust to change. Because of a woman's emotional identity with people and places around her, she needs more time to adjust to change that may affect her relationships. A man can logically deduce the benefits of a change and get "psyched-up" for it in a matter of minutes. Not so with a woman. Since she focuses on immediate consequences of relocating, for example, she needs time to overcome the initial adjustment before warming up to the advantages of it."[3]

Men and women find self-worth in different ways. A man finds his value in his job or profession. He does not depend on relationships for his sense of worth. Even his marriage relationship is not essential to his self-respect. His wife does play an important role as companion and lover, but a man's sense of worth comes from the reputation he earns on the job. A woman, especially one who is a homemaker, does not have the same focus outside the home. Her household duties will not win her the respect of others outside the home. She may become more isolated and will find self-worth in the respect and love given to her by her husband and family. In addition a woman's sense of worth is affected by her menstrual cycle. As her estrogen level fluctuates, so does her mood. Dr. Dobson notes, "Let's reduce it to an over simplification: men derive self-esteem by being respected; women feel worthy when they are loved. This may be the most important personality distinction between the sexes."[4]

A man finds his value in his job or profession.
He does not depend on relationships for his sense of worth.

Isn't it interesting to note here that Paul instructs husbands, "Love your wives, just as Christ loved the church" (Ephesians 5:25)? A husband's love brings self-worth and satisfaction to his wife. Paul also says, "Wives, submit to your husbands as to the Lord" (Ephesians 5:22). A wife's submission shows respect for her husband; it brings him a sense of worth and value. Husbands help build the self-esteem of their wives; wives in turn build self-esteem in their husbands. We complement each other rather than compete with each other.

Physical differences

Besides the obvious physical differences, there are more subtle physiological differences. Knowing them can bring a better understanding of the differences between men and women.

Dr. Paul Popenoe, the late founder of the American Institute of Family Relations in Los Angeles, wrote a brief article, "Are Women Really Different?" in which he lists differences between the sexes. Here is his list:

- Men and women differ in every cell of their bodies. The difference in the chromosome combination is the basic cause of development into maleness and femaleness.
- A woman has greater constitutional vitality, perhaps because of this chromosome difference. In the United States a woman normally outlives a man by three or four years.
- Men and women differ in their basic metabolism. The woman's being normally lower than that of a man.
- Men and women differ in skeletal structure. Women have a shorter head, broader face, less protruding chin, shorter legs and trunk. Men's teeth generally last longer than women's.
- A woman has a larger stomach, kidneys, liver, appendix, and smaller lungs.
- A woman has several important functions that are lacking in a man—menstruation, pregnancy, and lactation. All of these influence a woman's behaviors and feelings. She has different hormones than a man does. A woman's thyroid is larger and more active. It enlarges during pregnancy but also during menstruation; it makes her more vulnerable to goiter and provides resistance to cold, but it contributes to emotional instability, which causes her to laugh and cry more easily. It is also associated with smooth skin and a relatively hairless body.

- A woman's blood contains more water and 20 percent fewer red cells. Since these cells supply oxygen to the body, she tires more easily and is more prone to faint.
- In brute strength, men are 50 percent above women.
- A woman's heart beats more rapidly (80 beats per minute verses 72 for men). Her blood pressure is ten points lower than a man's. She has much less tendency toward high blood pressure at least until after menopause.
- A woman's breathing power is lower by a 7:10 ratio.
- A woman withstands higher temperatures better than a man.[5]

Sexual differences

Most marriage manuals outline the differences in sexual desire between men and women. A woman needs emotional and mental preparation for sexual intercourse. A man is stimulated more quickly and needs little or no preparation. Romantic words, actions (such as flowers or other kindnesses), and touch mean more to a woman than to a man. He is stimulated more by sight than she is. A woman's sexual drive is related to her menstrual cycle, but a man's remains fairly constant.

A woman's orientation toward relationships has a significant influence on her view of sex. Harsh or abusive treatment distorts the relationship. Abuse—verbal or physical—suppresses a woman's desire for sexual intimacy for days at a time. Because her emotions have been trampled by her husband, she is often repulsed by his sexual advances. She cannot understand how he could be interested in sex when the relationship is broken. Many women feel like prostitutes when they are forced to make love while feeling resentment toward their husbands. Harsh treatment does not depress a man's sexual drive in the same way. Failure to understand the differences between right-brain and left-brain orientation and how it affects sexual attitudes may lead to many conflicts in marriage.

Abuse—verbal or physical—suppresses a woman's desire for sexual intimacy for days at a time.

Intuitive differences

Perhaps another little phrase comes to mind here: a woman's intuition. Is there such a thing? What is it? Why is it a *woman's* intuition and not a *man's*? Well, there is such a thing as intuition. It is not some mystical insight given to women. Instead it is an unconscious perception of details that leads a woman to a conclusion about something. Sometimes a woman cannot give a specific explanation as to why she feels the way she feels, but she does feel a particular way. Men rely on logical analysis of circumstances and people's behavior and are often not aware of this intuition.

A woman often has a greater awareness of how to develop a loving relationship. She is sensitive and considerate of the feelings of her husband and others. She understands the impact of words and actions at an emotional level, which her husband often does not. A woman wants to be a lover, friend, and appreciated partner as much as he wants a sexual partnership, and she is often enthusiastic about developing such a meaningful multilevel relationship.

A woman wants to be a lover, friend, and appreciated partner as much as he wants a sexual partnership, and she is often enthusiastic about developing such a meaningful multilevel relationship.

A man often is unaware of this emotional intuition and must rely on skills and knowledge acquired from observation and experience. If his only example of relationships comes from his own childhood home and that relationship was dysfunctional, he will be handicapped in his ability to develop a meaningful relationship. Smalley observes, "Most men enter marriage knowing everything about sex and very little about genuine unselfish love."[6] Men do not generally have the intuitive awareness of how to deal with relationships, even the special relationship created by marriage. Here the miracle of God's love can provide a wonderful pattern. Paul wrote, "Husbands, love your wives, just as Christ loved the church and gave himself up for her" (Ephesians 5:25). Understanding the love of Christ for sinners can help a man overcome his emotional deficiencies. The sacrificing love of Christ is a pattern of love for others and, as Paul says, especially for husbands.

Men do not generally have the intuitive awareness
of how to deal with relationships,
even the special relationship created by marriage.

Conclusion

After reading about the differences between men and women, you can see that understanding these differences is extremely important as you relate to your spouse. It is a wise husband or wife who becomes more and more aware of these differences. In his Word, God provides some important distinctions in the roles he reveals for men and women.

Husbands, God has given you a very important role as servant/leader. Serve God first; then serve your wife and children by doing all you can do to meet their material, spiritual, and emotional needs. Be the leader in showing your wife and children more of what Jesus is all about. Love them as Christ loved us all. Sacrifice for them because you love them, as Christ sacrificed for you and all sinners. As you serve the needs of your wife by loving her through your words and actions, as you provide a positive role model for your children, your wife and children will respect you as their leader. In that kind of loving, nurturing, and respectful environment, love can permeate to the very core of your marriage and your relationship with your children.

Wives, God has given you an important role as a companion, specially suited to your husband. Serve your Savior first because of all he has done for you. Then respond to your husband in the same way, showing him respect and admiration. You need your husband's love; your husband needs your respect. You are the emotional hub of the home. You love intu-itively and deeply.

Together you can support each other by following God's sim-ple directions, but you can destroy the marriage by abandoning God's directions. Your relationship is not a competition. Com-petition in a marriage breeds jealousy, anger, and resentment. Marriage is better viewed as a blending of strengths. Such a blending will minimize the weaknesses—whatever they are and whoever has them.

Imagine an afternoon thunderstorm unexpectedly coming out of the southwest. In a matter of minutes, the skies darken, the wind intensifies, and sheets of rain pelt the roof and win-dows. In the aftermath, numerous branches, twigs, and leaves are lying on the lawn. The storm is an object lesson of what storms of conflict can do in marriage relationships.

While the storm is raging, those involved in the conflict can feel hurt, anger, and a sense of hopelessness. They may think, "Can anything good come from this?" God can use storms as an opportunity to enrich relationships; to produce new branches of commitment and love, which can generate, by God's grace, new leaves of understanding, respect, kindness, and caring. As you experience storms in your marriage, don't let Satan lead you to think that God is not interested in your problems. God cares about you and your marriage. Turn to him! Trust him! Lean on him! He, in his wisdom, may allow storms to clear out all the debris of the past so new branches can grow and new leaves can appear.

Storms don't have to be fatal to your marriage. Remember Betty and Dan. They were ready to abandon the ship of mar-riage. But there is hope in the miracle of God's love. You may need the help of your pastor or a Christian counselor, but God can use them as his instruments of healing.

What happened to Betty and Dan?

Both Betty and Dan went to their pastor and honestly shared their marital problems. Their pastor referred them to a Chris-tian counselor. In the counseling process, Dan became more aware of Betty's need to be loved, wanted, and appreciated. As

Dan, more each day, showed through his words and actions that Betty was, next to God, the most important thing in his life, Betty responded by showing more respect toward Dan. Betty began to feel more secure in the relationship. Dan took the time to listen to Betty when she spoke to him. Betty heard the unspoken message of his listening. Dan showed what he felt: I really do care about you.

Over the course of time, as Betty and Dan continued to be more respectful and considerate of each others' needs and feelings, both felt the desire to pray for each other and with each other. Betty and Dan found that the feelings of love for each other were revitalized. As God came more and more into Betty and Dan's life, both reported that their relationship was becoming the best it had ever been.

Dan learned the skills to better meet Betty's need to be loved. Betty responded to Dan's leadership by respecting him as her husband and the father of their children.

EXERCISES

1. Sit down with your spouse; discuss one thing you have learned from this chapter. Did your spouse learn the same thing? If you each learned something different, explore the reason why.

2. Make a list of the differences between you and your spouse. How can the differences complement one another?

3. Wives, consider one thing your husband does that has gained your respect. Tell him!

4. Husbands, find one way, other than sexually, that you can show love and affection for your wife. Do it and repeat it!

CHAPTER 4

The Miracle of Oneness

Several years ago a small book carried the title *One Plus One*. As you might guess, the book was a discussion of marriage. I have always remembered the title because it captures God's mathematical principle for marriage. God's plan for a Christian marriage combines one man and one women to equal one harmonious unit—one plus one equals one. To human reason that seems inconceivable. We have come to value personal identity above everything else. We assume that a relationship is good as long as it does not demand too much of us. In addition, so many married couples do not experience the unity and harmony of God's design. For them one plus one means tension and territorial battles. Yet God established marriage as a special relationship in which both husband and wife can find true joy and happiness in each other. One plus one will equal one.

Impossible? God's ways always seem strange to our human minds. God reminds us, "As the heavens are higher than the earth, so are my ways higher than your ways and my thoughts than your thoughts" (Isaiah 55:9). A simple example is what God reveals about himself. He says that he is triune, Father, Son, and Holy Spirit. God's mathematics here is simple: one plus one plus one equals one, not three. He is three persons, yet one Lord God. We cannot understand this truth about the essence of God, yet by the Spirit's power we believe it to be true. We accept it because God says so.

God's plan for marriage is oneness

About marriage, God says, "a man will . . . be united to his wife, and they will become one flesh" (Genesis 2:24). Jesus repeated the concept when he talked about marriage, "So they are no longer two, but one. Therefore what God has joined together, let man not separate" (Matthew 19:6). Certainly the oneness between a man and a wife in marriage is not the same as the mystery of the Trinity, the truth that God is one, yet three. Nevertheless, making one out of two, a man and a woman in marriage, is much more than just a reference to the sexual union. God intends for marriage to reflect the miracle of oneness. "One flesh" applies to sharing goals for married life, matching priorities with what God says is important, pursuing heaven through Jesus Christ together, and creating an intimacy where two individuals can blend their hopes, dreams, talents, temperaments, and concerns into one.

Making one out of two, a man and a woman in marriage, is much more than just a reference to the sexual union.

No one can nurture oneness when he or she pursues individual and personal interests while neglecting the interests of the marriage partner. A young couple came to my office seeking counseling and help. Both freely admitted that their marriage seemed empty and unfulfilling. More than that, they just didn't seem to talk heart to heart any more. As a preliminary exercise I had both of them fill out a time chart for an average week. With both working two different jobs, including frequent overtime, labor alone ate up 90 to 100 hours a week. In addition, the husband was very active in recreational sports. Three nights a week, he left his wife at home and participated in some activity. Add in commuting, household chores, sleeping, and what is left? Oneness in marriage takes much more effort than saying "I do" at the altar. Oneness in marriage is a lifelong effort to push self-interest into the background.

How does God achieve oneness in marriage?

The first thing God does through his Word is to open our eyes to see things as he sees them. God isn't satisfied with the outward impression; he looks deeper into our hearts. There God sees just how dirty and sinful every heart is. He sees what destroys marriages and fights against oneness. Among the sins God finds within each of us is pride and selfishness. Those sins have risen within the hearts of people as far back as Adam and Eve. They first appeared in Satan, who wanted to be number one. When he turned against God and was thrown out of heaven, he wanted nothing better than to disrupt God's perfect creation. So he disguised himself and spoke to Eve. When Eve told Satan that she would die if she ate of the forbidden fruit, Satan countered, "You will not surely die. . . . For God knows that when you eat of it your eyes will be opened, and you will be like God, knowing good and evil" (Genesis 3:4,5). When Satan said "You will be like God!" he encouraged Eve to repeat the same sin he had committed in heaven. Satan wanted Eve to assert herself. Let me paraphrase his words, "Eve, be number one. You can't really be happy unless you come first. Never mind what God says. Do what you want. God's threats are just an attempt to keep you down. You won't really die."

Pride is and remains at the root of every rebellion against the Lord God and his Word. It also has the potential to destroy a marriage. Pride and selfishness lead us to assert our rights and wants in the marriage relationship and to minimize love, consideration, and sacrifice. Soon our pride speeds us down the "me first" highway. If we continue down that road, unhappiness, conflict, and perhaps even divorce lie ahead. That's not what God wants for any marriage. In order to get us on a different road, God opens our eyes to see the sin within us. His law shouts out that pride and selfishness are sins, damning sins, sins that destroy the relationship with God and relationships with other humans. It is wrong to say "me first" when it comes to deciding how to spend money, or assert "me first" when you plan to use free time, or even to demand "me first" in the number of times a couple makes love. Scripture urges us to recognize the deadly sin and to repent. "As surely as I live, declares the Sovereign LORD, I take no pleasure in the death of the wicked, but rather that they turn from their ways and live. Turn! Turn from your evil ways! Why will you die?" (Ezekiel 33:11).

Pride and selfishness lead us to assert our rights and wants in the marriage relationship
and to minimize love, consideration, and sacrifice.

This discussion of selfishness might strike you as rather simplistic when talking about the myriad of problems that plague a marriage. The list of problems includes communication failures, abusive behavior, anger and violence, arguments over money, sexual difficulties, discipline of children, and on and on. Every couple has its own unique and troublesome issues that need to be resolved. But most often those issues are only symptoms that grow from the root sin of "me first." So it has been ever since the garden. Before a couple can honestly and effectively work toward resolving other problems, both have to see the underlying need to repent over their selfishness.

Sin and grace

God's Word does not stop with identifying the problem. It clearly and wonderfully presents the solution as well. We are helpless to solve the guilt of sin or to overcome its effects in any significant way. God's solution is one that we would have never imagined and could never manufacture. Before the first sin in the garden, God planned to overcome that sin and all others by sending his one and only Son, Jesus, to die for all humanity. The good news of the gospel of Jesus as Savior proclaims that God has done everything necessary to remove the guilt of sin and to reverse the punishment each of us so richly deserves. The gospel shines as a warm, magnetic light from the cross of Jesus Christ. Through the message of the cross, God draws us away from our pride and selfishness and draws us closer to himself.

How different the cross of Christ is from the attitudes of human society and of those in our own hearts. At the cross we do not see selfishness or a me-first attitude. Instead we see genuine love, complete compassion, and total commitment. "This is love: not that we loved God, but that he loved us and sent his Son as an atoning sacrifice for our sins" (1 John 4:10). At the cross, we see God put us first by punishing his own Son for our misdeeds. "God demonstrates his own love for us in this: While we were still sinners, Christ died for us" (Romans 5:8).

We need to go to that cross for the assurance of our own forgiveness and eternal life. In addition, the cross also is the hard and enduring foundation for our marriage. Because the gospel of the cross is God's love, it provides the purest example of love and gives spiritual power to change our pride and selfishness. The gospel of Jesus is the most important tool Christ gives Christian spouses to make one plus one equal one. Paul says, "Your attitude should be the same as that of Christ Jesus: Who, being in very nature God, did not consider equality with God something to be grasped, but made himself nothing, taking the very nature of a servant, being made in human likeness. And being found in appearance as a man, he humbled himself and became obedient to death—even death on a cross!" (Philippians 2:5-8). Let's briefly examine the attitude of Christ, for there we see the practical ways to build and restore what was once destroyed and separated.

We need to go to that cross for the assurance of our own forgiveness and eternal life. In addition, the cross also is the hard and enduring foundation for our marriage.

Christ did not demand to be first, but made himself nothing. He gave himself up totally to the Father's will, just as he prayed in another garden. "Yet not what I will, but what you will" (Mark 14:36). Christ submitted to the Father's plan even when it meant his suffering and death. Christ became a servant, a slave. Think of how he did the slave's job by washing the dirty feet of the disciples on Maundy Thursday. He humbled himself to become obedient to death and gave up his life. Humility and submission are characteristics of Jesus. He gave up his throne of absolute power and majesty to come to earth and live under his Father's law in place of sinners who could not live as God demanded. Christ carried our sins and was punished in our place, because our sins cry out for punishment and damnation. Christ became our substitute and suffered all the punishment, all the wrath a just God decreed, for our sins.

What does this have to do with marriage?

Good question. First, Jesus brings us back to God. Now we are acceptable to the Father through the blood of his Son. Because of Jesus, we are restored to the Father. As a part of God's family, we experience that wonderful family relationship that Adam and Eve had once known in the garden. We have oneness with the Father through Jesus. Listen to Christ's beautiful prayer and his desire for our lives. "My prayer is not for them alone. I pray also for those who will believe in me through their message, that all of them may be one, Father, just as you are in me and I am in you. May they also be in us so that the world may believe that you have sent me. I have given them the glory that you gave me, that they may be one as we are one: I in them and you in me. May they be brought to complete unity to let the world know that you sent me and have loved them even as you have loved me" (John 17:20-23).

What Christ did has repaired our relationship with God. That is the heart and core of healing any relationship. Before we can truly bridge broken relationships with our spouses, our children, or our neighbors, we need to understand clearly what Jesus did to bridge our relationship with God. Because of our sins, including our sins of pride and selfishness, we totally destroyed our relationship with God. Not only did we destroy that relationship, but by nature we also did not even want to repair it. But Jesus came and rebuilt the relationship with God through his innocent life and death. His blood repaired the chasm between God and man.

Before we can truly bridge broken relationships with our spouses, our children, or our neighbors, we need to understand clearly what Jesus did to bridge our relationship with God.

Once we understand that Jesus restored our broken relationship with God, we can begin to fix our relationships with other people. Here's God's perspective on our relationships with others, "This is how God showed his love among us: He sent his one and only Son into the world that we might live through him. . . . Dear friends, since God so loved us, we also ought to love one another" (1 John 4:9,11). Notice how Jesus fixed our relationship with his Father. He did not use might or force. He did not use manipulation or bargaining. Jesus used himself up totally. In a word, he fixed our relationship with God by loving us and expressing that love in his humility, service, obedience, submission, and sacrifice. By his effort he brought us back into the family of God and made us one again with our God. Love is also necessary to build any lasting and genuine relationship between humans. When spouses express love in humility, service, obedience, submission, and sacrifice, they can build the miracle of oneness in their marriages.

Of course, the world around us does not try to solve broken marriages in the same way. Some approaches suggest that spouses should first "find themselves." Others advise battling marriage partners "to express your anger honestly; let it all come out." Still others seek to repair marriage relationships by telling spouses, "First love yourself. Then you can really love another." Don't try to use the tools that the world thinks are appropriate. All of these attempts are nothing more than a smoke screen for selfishness. If we try to use these tools to solve problems, the results will be devastating. We understand true love by looking at the love of God in Christ. When we understand his love, we know the pattern and have the strength to love others as he loved us. God's Word is the toolbox from which we draw the tools necessary to build a successful marriage. Let's turn to the toolbox, where God shows us how to build the miracle of oneness in marriage. Open it to Ephesians chapter 5.

Scripture's specific instructions on building the miracle of oneness

> Submit to one another out of reverence for Christ.
>
> Wives, submit to your husbands as to the Lord. For the husband is the head of the wife as Christ is the head of the church, his body, of which he is the Savior. Now as the church submits to Christ, so also wives should submit to their husbands in everything.
>
> Husbands love your wives, just as Christ loved the church and gave himself up for her to make her holy, cleansing her by the washing with water through the word, and to present her to himself as a radiant church, without stain or wrinkle or any other blemish, but holy and blameless. In this same way, husbands ought to love their wives as their own bodies. He who loves his wife loves himself. After all, no one ever hated his own body, but he feeds and cares for it, just as Christ does the church—for we are members of his body. "For this reason a man will leave his father and mother and be united to his wife, and the two will become one flesh." This is a profound mystery—but I am talking about Christ and the church. However, each one of you also must love his wife as he loves himself, and the wife must respect her husband. (Ephesians 5:21-33)

The above section from Ephesians 5 is the apostle's inspired marriage manual for the miracle of oneness. Portions of this section are often heard at weddings. Unfortunately, in our day and setting, these verses also kindle the ire of many who view them as some outdated, patriarchal arrangement. Nothing, however, could be farther from the truth. Notice, first of all, that Paul begins the section by saying, "Submit to one another out of reverence for Christ." Submission is a way of life for Christians because we follow the one who is perfect in submission. Jesus our Savior lived in submission to the needs of others. He fed the hungry, healed the ill or crippled, hugged the children, comforted those in grief, taught small groups and large crowds, and even washed feet. Submission to the needs of others is not a nasty concept for a disciple of the Savior. In the Old Testament, the Messiah is called the servant of the Lord. *Submit* is a word that means "to arrange under the orders of another." It calls to mind the ranks upon ranks of soldiers that answer to the command of an officer. Jesus arranged his life under the will of the Father and under the needs of sinners. "The Son of Man did not come to be served, but to serve, and to give his life as a ransom for many" (Matthew 20:28).

Submit is a word that God also assigns to the Christian wife. "Wives, submit to your husbands as to the Lord. For the husband is the head of the wife as Christ is the head of the church, his body, of which he is the Savior. Now as the church submits to Christ, so also wives should submit to their husbands in everything" (Ephesians 5:22-24). The submission of a wife is freely given, not something coerced or demanded. No one can make a Christian wife submit, because her submission flows from her freedom in Jesus Christ. That is reflected in the phrase "as to the Lord." Paul is not saying that the husband is the Lord. Jesus is the Lord, and the wife's submission is a fruit of faith that reflects her love to the Lord Jesus. She is willing to live to his glory in how she lives in her relationship with her husband.

> *The submission of a wife is freely given,*
> *not something coerced or demanded.*

But before a husband can sit back and say "I'm the boss," the apostle goes on to say, "Husbands, love your wives, just as Christ loved the church and gave himself up for her." The husband is the head of the wife only in the same way as Christ is the head of the church. Jesus, as the church's head, is not a domineering master, but the one who is accountable to the needs of others.

The husband is to love as Jesus loved; he is to display an unconditional one-way love that follows the pattern of the love Christ displayed to the whole world.

The Greek word used in the passage from Ephesians is a special word for love. As God defines this word, it has nothing to do with emotional closeness, sexual attraction, or physical affection. The word here for love is a word that reflects God's very essence. It denotes a decision to act humbly and in service to the needs of another. It is the very same word used in John 3:16: "God so loved the world that he gave his one and only Son." God challenges a Christian husband to love his wife by deciding to act humbly and in service to her. He loves his wife as Christ loves the church, in humility, sacrifice, service, and obedience to the will of the Father. In this Christian context then, submission on the part of a wife actually brings her total liberation. Her husband is commanded by God always to put her needs, her wants, and her feelings above his own, just as Christ did for the church.

God challenges a Christian husband to love his wife by deciding to act humbly and in service to her.

If Christ is the top priority in a husband's life, how can he show this image of Christ to his wife? Let's get specific. In the First Commandment God tells us that he is to be number one in our lives. Then God tells husbands in Ephesians 5 that the wife comes next. The Christian man is to reflect Jesus Christ and be a servant to the needs of others—his wife, his children, his neighbors. The husband will never demand love from his wife, coerce submission, or force respect. Jesus never forced anyone to follow him. Jesus simply loved us, served us, and died for us. His love prompts our following. "We love because he first loved us" (1 John 4:19). So it is with the husband/wife relationship. Is it possible for a man to live exactly like Christ? Of course not, because every man is still a sinner who displays that sin in countless selfish ways. Yet the Word of God works wonders and miracles. The Holy Spirit brings a man to faith through the gospel and changes not only the heart but also the habits. By the Holy Spirit's power, a man can follow the pattern of Christ's love. God works this miracle through his Word of grace. Therefore, this love that creates a oneness is not based on some emotional feeling. Feelings are unstable and change minute by minute. Therefore it is obvious that God wants the miracle of this oneness based upon Christ's love.

> *The husband will never demand love from his wife,*
> *coerce submission, or force respect.*

Love: a decision prompted by the Spirit—NOT a feeling

Any couple that has been married more than a month realizes how emotions shift faster than the stock market. But love that creates the miracle of oneness is that special love that follows the pattern of Christ's love. As a husband, I might not always feel close to my wife, but by the Spirit's power I have decided to live a life that puts her first above my needs. This decision is possible only by the Spirit's working through God's Word. When a Christian man says "I will," he says it not just to his wife. First and foremost he says "I will" to his Savior and God. "I will live according to your Holy Word. I will live your love of service, sacrifice, and humility. I will put my wife first just as you put me and all the world first. I will put my wife first in how I use my time, my energy, and my spending habits. I will live for her, be ready to die for her, regardless of how she treats me." Wow! That's quite a lot, isn't it? And before the skeptics shake their heads in disbelief, the Christian man knows to look to Jesus for the strength and ability to live this kind of love. With Paul he confesses, "I can do everything through him who gives me strength" (Philippians 4:13).

Not many men today know how to be a man as God defines manhood. But Christians look to Jesus Christ. He showed his power in serving and giving. His actions show every man that compassion is not unmanly. He did not seek to be first or best to prove his manhood. Instead he demonstrated that humility is not weakness. Real strength is not in a "might-makes-right" or "macho" attitude but rather in one that quietly and confidently reveals, "I have the might to do what is right."

The result is that the wife is moved to a renewed commitment to live for her husband. More and more she seeks to please the one who has demonstrated that she is number one in his life. More and more she lives to bring him joy, as he lives for her. She shows him respect. She willingly submits to his leadership. This too is a miracle of the Spirit's work through the Word. She does so not because she is inferior or a possession. She is a treasured equal who submits as Christ submitted to his heavenly Father. Because she believes in the redeeming love of Jesus, she lives as he reveals in his Word. She submits to her husband as she submits to the Lord. Just as a Christian husband loves Christ because Christ loved us first, so also a wife loves her husband all the more, and grows in that love, when her husband loves her first. She thrives in her husband's love; he thrives in her respect and submission. Together they become one through the interplay of love and submission. Instead of breeding conflict over who's better or first, they complement each other and treasure each other for what they are.

She thrives in her husband's love;

he thrives in her respect and submission.

Together they become one

through the interplay of love and submission.

This miracle of oneness starts with the gospel of Jesus Christ, the freeing power of his love. Christ never demanded; he gave. Christ never forced; he served. Christ never asked; he delivered. So too the Christian husband, by the Spirit's power, lives that love of Jesus. A Christian husband never forces love or insists on submission. Only when he lives the love of sacrifice will the wife respond. She is his helper, who was created suitable for him and given to him by God. He, on the other hand, lives his love to cherish her as that special creation from God to him. Then, and only then, two become one.

The miracle of oneness even through our differences

So often I hear couples say, "We have nothing in common anymore. How can we build a happy marriage if we don't share common interests or hobbies?" I truly believe that such thinking is overplayed. God has made each gender different, as we talked about in a previous chapter. God wants us to relish and nurture the differences for the good of the union.

Think of two pieces of a plaque. Each may be brightly colored, each may be pleasing to look at, each may be suitable to hang up by itself. Yet it is only when the two pieces are brought together do you see the complete message of the plaque, the total picture of how the colors and the pattern interrelate. God wants us to appreciate the way he made us—different so we can complement one another.

That means that the husband, as the head of the wife, is bound by God's will to encourage his wife to develop all the gifts, abilities, and interests she might possess from God's gracious hand. God has made her and gifted her, and the more the husband sees her abilities used, the greater the good for the union. At the same time, the wife will not try to change and mold her husband into the man she might want him to be. She will rejoice in how God made him and gifted him. Rather than marriage dulling our personal abilities and unique individuality, it serves to highlight and nurture the special gifts each spouse has. For only then can we fully experience what blessings God would pour out upon us through the union.

Real communication among Christians is a sincere effort to understand the other person.

The differences are vital to developing the whole marriage. Talk about and explore your differences in outlook, in interests, in abilities. True communication in a Christian marriage is not an attempt to make sure the speaker is understood. Following the definition of love that comes from the cross, real communication among Christians is a sincere effort to understand the other person. What is my spouse thinking? What is my spouse feeling? This communication is a constant part of a growing marriage, because marriages never stay the same. We all grow as we live through new and different experiences. We grow older. We change as children enter the home and we develop parenting skills. We change when the children leave or when career or work alter our lives. Illnesses or hardships force us to adapt. Communication is a day-to-day effort to understand the needs, anxieties, and concerns of my spouse. If I am first interested in knowing how the other feels, then I am not so concerned about explaining myself all the time. The desire to know what the other person is thinking and feeling leads to genuine "soul-to-soul" communication.

EXERCISES

1. Pick the best statement. Then discuss with your spouse why you picked as you did.

   "I got married to be happy."

   "I got married to make someone happy."

2. When was the last time you felt especially close to your spouse? What happened? Did you do something that contributed to bringing about that feeling of closeness? What did you do? Duplicate those efforts today, regardless of how you think your spouse might respond.

3a. For husbands: Ask your wife for specific things you can do that would make her feel special and treasured. Start with one thing or make a list, and love by doing for her those things that she treasures.

3b. For wives: Ask your husband for specific things you can do that will help build your relationship. Start with one thing or make a list, and serve your husband by doing for him the things he likes.

4. Practice praying out loud together. Thank Jesus for the unique abilities of your spouse, and ask the Savior for help to change specific weaknesses in yourself.

CHAPTER 5:

Indicators of a Marriage Headed for Trouble

We all have been there. A young bride, wearing a dress she carefully selected for her wedding, walks down the aisle, escorted by her father. Her attendants have already gone ahead of her and await her at the altar with her future husband and his attendants. The organ, the flowers, the dresses all contribute to the festive and happy moment in the lives of both bride and groom. Perhaps all the details are not always the same, but we all have been at wedding ceremonies where a young woman and a young man publicly begin their life together.

What a wonderful scene! The day has taken hours of planning and more than a little money to complete. Families and friends gather in God's house to listen as the bride and groom pledge their love, faithfulness, and commitment to each other. The couple exchange rings, receive the blessing of God, and walk down the center aisle to receive the congratulations and best wishes of their guests. After the church service and reception, they embark on their new life together. Each one enters marriage with the hope of a long and fulfilling relationship.

What happened on the road to happily ever after?

For some couples, their wedding day is a day they still cherish. Every year married couples celebrate the day of their wedding with some special event. Perhaps it's just dinner and a movie or maybe it's only a card, but we do celebrate anniversaries. Special anniversaries call for special parties.

For some, however, that day may be one they would just as soon forget. It is sad to note that while millions of men and women can fall in love, millions can also end their marriages. These couples may have experienced the same service as the couple above, but they did not live happily ever after. Statistics reveal the problems in reaching the hope of marital happiness. Depending on the source, almost every other marriage is headed for trouble. What happens?

A case study: Steven and Susan

Kathy, age 15, and John, age 13, sat motionless and quiet. They stared at the floor, then looked at each other, seeking answers. Finally they turned to their parents who sat on the couch on the other side of the room. Kathy and John are the children of Steven and Susan, who had been experiencing marital difficulties for years. They had separated several months before. After 16 years of marriage, Steven and Susan had reached the point of telling their children the marriage was over. They told Kathy and John, "We are getting a divorce!"

After 16 years of marriage,
Steven and Susan had reached the point
of telling their children the marriage was over.

What could the children say? Kathy and John were encouraged to share what they were feeling. Before Kathy responded, tears began rolling down her cheeks. After what seemed an eternity of silence, Kathy said, "I'm afraid." After another pause, "I'm worried. What is going to happen to our family—to John and me and to you, Mom and Dad?" Another pause, "Where will we live? Who will we live with? Will John and I have to leave our school, our friends, our home?"

John's response was shorter but just as deeply felt: "Why, Mom and Dad? I don't understand this! Everything seems to be falling apart." Then he buried his head in his hands. His emotions gave way, and he could not hold back his tears.

John's response raises a question we might all have. How does it happen that two people come to the end of their married life together? How can two people who once felt so much affection for one another come to the realization that their relationship cannot be repaired? How does indifference, anger, and perhaps even loathing replace love? Divorce torments the hearts of children, teenagers, and even adults. It seizes those hearts and squeezes out hope, while tearing apart relationships. Those affected by divorce plunge into a sea of doubt, confusion, fear, lack of trust, and insecurity. The marriage is over; it will not work. The family is gone. Divorce is such a final word that it can literally tear a child's or a teenager's world apart.

Steven and Susan did not intend to bring such pain and instability into the lives of their children. They did not plan to cause each other pain or enter the chaos of establishing a new life without the other. As they looked at their children, perhaps they had the sense they were mutilating a family and changing their future permanently. No matter what they had intended or planned, the divorce brought pain.

What happened to Steven and Susan's marriage? How did the love they felt on their wedding day escape them? Over the 16 years of their marriage, Susan sensed a steady decline in her relationship with Steven. They dated in high school and became high-school sweethearts. A year after they graduated, they were married. Shortly after they married, Steven started his own business. Susan admitted that Steven was a hard worker: "He had a knack for business." But, from Susan's perspective, Steven became so involved in wanting to make his business successful that there wasn't any time for her. When Steven came home, he was too tired to go out for dinner and a movie. Because Steven worked literally seven days a week, Susan went to church alone. When Kathy and John were born, Susan devoted herself to being a mother.

Steven's perception of the 16 years of married life was somewhat different. He felt unappreciated by his wife. Steven believed that the time and effort he was investing in his business was for the financial security of Susan and his children. He thought that Susan should have understood that. But Susan felt she had been left virtually on her own to raise the children. She had taken them to church. She had said their prayers with them and had taken care of their Christian training.

However, as time passed and with the lack of Steven's support, encouragement, and leadership, Susan admitted that she had become lonely and discouraged. Susan began attending church with her children less frequently. She excused herself by saying, "If Steven doesn't care, why should I?" Susan felt isolated from Steven. She expressed her need to feel loved, wanted, and appreciated by her husband. To fill that void, that emptiness inside her, Susan purchased a lot of things for the house, the children, and herself. Yet Steven never acknowledged how beautiful the home looked or how nice she and the children looked. Unfortunately, Susan charged most of the purchases on their credit card.

During this time, Steven's business was growing. As the business grew, he became a better provider. Steven felt he deserved some pleasurable things for himself as well. So Steven purchased a new boat and a truck. He reasoned that the business could absorb the cost, and he could use the boat to invite friends and prospective customers for some time on the lake. Both were shocked to discover that with his charges, together with Susan's purchases, they were getting "in over their heads" financially.

Susan and Steven began to react negatively to each other. Steven felt he deserved more respect from Susan because he was working so hard to provide for the finer things of life. In view of their financial problems, Steven chose to spend more time with the business. Susan complained that Steven was never around, but he would rationalize his time away from his family as the only way to take care of the bills. Steven became more critical of Susan's misuse of the credit card. At one point Steven cut up the card so Susan couldn't use it. This caused Susan to feel even more alienated and distant from him.

More and more, Steven sensed that Susan was pulling away from him. Steven started feeling the loneliness and lack of interest that Susan had been feeling for years. To fill his loneliness, Steven started spending more time with friends at the local cocktail lounge. His friends were there for him. He could tell them, and they understood, just how Susan was treating him. The relationship with Susan began to degenerate. As he withdrew from her, she withdrew from him, only causing him to draw farther away and leading her to move even farther away. More and more they isolated themselves from each other. They avoided conversation because they didn't have anything to talk about. If they did talk, it usually ended in an argument.

Susan finally said to the counselor, "I just can't take it anymore. I am totally unhappy as Steven's wife. I care for Steven, but I don't love him as a husband. Somewhere along the line, my feelings for Steven died. He thinks the only reason I exist is to supply him with food, sex, clean clothes, a clean house, and clean kids. I've got to get out of this relationship before I lose my mind."

Steven said, "After so many years of her not appreciating what I am trying to accomplish, I've had it! If only she would show some interest in the business. She avoids me. She doesn't seem to be interested in meeting my needs as a man. I don't know; the spark just isn't there anymore. I think it would be best if we got a divorce so I could just get on with my life; Susan, with hers. It's not right for Kathy and John either. Susan and I walk around on eggshells; the kids don't need to hear our arguing."

What happens to the children? Contrary to what others may say, time does not heal the wounds of children whose parents are divorced. Divorce is as devastating to children as it is to parents. Emotional development in children is directly related to a warm, secure, stable, and nurturing environment. This starts with a mother and father's marriage relationship and how they model that to their children. Sadly, Kathy and John were not experiencing a warm, nurturing, stable, and secure environment. They felt a sense of loss, which brought fear and uncertainty. Children often feel that they may have done something wrong to cause Mom and Dad's divorce; they feel responsible for the failure of the marriage and family. In addition, they often feel rejected by their parents. Because parents reject each other as spouses, the children often feel that their parents are rejecting and abandoning them.

Divorce is as devastating to children as it is to parents.

This case history is a real one. The details emphasize many problems that surface in other marriages. Many of the problems can be overcome before they reach the point where divorce seems to be the only answer. Even though, since the 1960s, divorce has become a more fashionable way of dealing with marriage difficulties, divorce is not the solution. It doesn't solve anything. What it does is set the stage for numerous other problems. Our approach in this book is to help spouses find solutions that will revitalize their relationship and help them avoid the possibility of divorce.

Ten indicators of a marriage in trouble

Could Steven and Susan have avoided divorce? Certainly. How? If they had been more aware of the symptoms, they may have been able to step out of the cycle of deterioration. If they knew the indicators that showed their marriage was heading for trouble, they might have been able to alter their patterns of behavior. If they could not resolve the problems on their own with God's help, they might have sought the help of their pastor and a Christian counselor. Then with God's help, guidance, and blessing, the marriage of Steven and Susan could have survived.

Couples who experience crises in their relationship exhibit a set of characteristics, symptoms, or indicators. Any single indicator can act as a cancerous growth that will cause more problems. If the problems are not diagnosed and treated, they can sap the love, commitment, and joy of a healthy marriage. Like with Susan and Steven, the problems will lead spouses away from each other and especially away from the means of grace. When couples drift away from the means of grace, that is, away from hearing God's Word and receiving Holy Communion, they drift away from the spiritual power to work toward a growing, healthy marriage.

A list of indicators has been developed for this book. While there are other indicators, these are listed because they are seen most often in troubled marriages. These indicators might be a good discussion starter for anyone having marital concerns. First, it can give those who are contemplating marriage a way to discuss marriage and ward off potential problems. It can also help those with a healthy marriage deepen their love and commitment. Finally, it can help those whose marriages need repair find a way to begin the diagnosis of the problems and move to find solutions.

1. A lack of spiritual oneness

Christian marriages have an advantage over other marriages because they have an additional, spiritual dimension. Christian spouses begin their married lives understanding God's undeserved love in Christ. Because husbands know the way that Christ loved the church and gave himself for it, they can love their wives in the same way. Because wives know the way all Christians submit to Jesus out of love and respect, they can follow that pattern in their relationship with their husbands. Since both know what forgiveness is all about, they can forgive each other. Whenever spouses pray the Lord's Prayer, they ask for the ability to forgive. Christians regularly petition, "and forgive us our sins as we forgive those who sin against us." And Christians understand that our heavenly Father designed and created marriage for our happiness here on earth. God knows exactly what is best for your marriage. He is the expert who can help.

This spiritual dimension has one more important advantage. God the Holy Spirit works within us when we use the means of grace. When a husband and wife attend church together regularly, study the Word together, and receive Holy Communion often, the Holy Spirit strengthens and nurtures faith. It's like being connected to a power source—a spiritual power source. Whenever believers avoid hearing the gospel or receiving Holy Communion, they disconnect from God's power to work within. Hearing and reading God's Word seems like something we can do without at times, but God promises to work through the gospel in Word and sacrament. He does not promise to work within us any other way.

Hearing and reading God's Word seems like something we can do without at times, but God promises to work through the gospel in Word and sacrament. He does not promise to work within us any other way.

What does this have to do with marriage? Remember Steven and Susan. Early in the marriage relationship, Steven decided that work and establishing a business was more important than worship. As the years went by, Susan struggled to maintain her contact with God through the Word and made a special effort to teach the children the importance of the gospel. But eventually, she also gave up her worship life. As a result, neither Steven nor Susan had the spiritual resources to deal with their deteriorating relationship. They had no spiritual oneness. But through the gospel the Holy Spirit equips spouses with the spiritual resources to enrich their marriage.

Many spouses adhere to different religious beliefs. A husband may belong to one church or to no church at all and a wife may belong to another or no church at all. In those situations, the believing spouse has a responsibility to continue to cling to God's gospel of forgiveness in Jesus by using the Word, privately if necessary, and by attending worship services, alone if necessary. The believing spouse has the opportunity to witness without arguing and through that witness to work on the heart of the unbelieving spouse. Whatever the situation, the believer must not "disconnect" from the power source—the gospel.

2. Not spending time alone with each other

When husbands get so involved in their work, businesses, hobbies, or other recreational, civic, or church activities, the wife can feel unloved, unneeded, and unappreciated. When a wife gets overly involved in the children, the house, her career, hobbies, recreational, civic, and church activities, the husband can feel that his wife does not respect him for what he is doing for her and the family. The result brings feelings of loneliness and isolation. The marriage is bound to suffer. In any marriage, spouses will drift apart unless they develop a plan to grow together and stay together.

Spouses must find a time to "turn off" the business, the kids, the activities, even the church activities, and to "turn on" each other. The courting or dating process does not end with marriage. That is just the beginning. Next to God, your spouse is your top priority. Spouses can go on dates without the kids or without friends, they can vacation together, take short weekend trips, or get involved in joint projects.

All too often we take our spouses for granted. As we get sucked into the business of everyday life, our schedules become tyrants, demanding time to go to meetings, shuttle the kids, go here or there, and do this or that. We sometimes get so committed that we don't have time for the most important person in our lives. Overcommitment leads to fatigue, stress, and exhaustion and can have a negative impact on any marriage. A woman is particularly vulnerable when her husband commits to too many things and has little or no time for her and the family.

In the case study earlier in this chapter, Steven dedicated himself to making his business successful. Every day of his week was either spent working or trying to find time to relieve the stress of work. He took no time for Susan. Then when the children came, he turned their training over to her. Susan learned to do things without Steven, and she felt frustrated and angry that they did not do things together. Eventually they could not do things together. Even their conversation was strained because they had nothing in common.

3. *Not enough space or distance in the relationship*

It is important to find time to do things together, but too much of a good thing will create other problems. When one spouse cannot allow some distance or "breathing room" for the other in the relationship, the other may sense a lack of trust. One spouse can feel suffocated by the other spouse. When a spouse cannot grant space to the other, it is usually a sign of jealousy or low self-esteem. Sometimes it comes from a desire to control another person. Jealousy, low self-esteem, and a need to control another person can undermine the relationship.

There is an old adage which illustrates that love must be given freely. It should not be coerced or demanded. It says, "If you have something and you let it go and it comes back, it is truly yours. If you have something that you let go and it doesn't come back, it was never yours to begin with." Unconditional love confidently gives the other spouse opportunities to do things alone or to spend time with friends or relatives apart from each other.

Marriages must balance togetherness and the need for separate space. Too much separation will destroy a marriage and too much of the wrong kind of togetherness will also create problems. Trust is the foundation of healthy marriages. Develop and strengthen that trust by granting each other some time apart without neglecting the time together.

Marriages must balance togetherness and the need for separate space.

4. Money problems

Believe it or not, most marital arguments are over money. When two people enter marriage with different philosophies about spending money, the potential for problems exists. One may spend freely, and the other may be more conservative about spending money. One may come from a family where the wife took care of all the financial affairs; another may come from a family where the husband handled all the money. These issues and others will create tension. A couple can minimize the possible problems by talking about their financial resources. Together they should decide who will pay the bills on a regular basis and how they will decide when and if to buy new appliances, a new car, a house, or anything else. Financial issues can cause friction which can lead to ongoing conflicts.

One way to discuss financial matters is to develop a budget. The budget will provide a financial plan for both husband and wife. It can minimize the arguments over money, as well as help both spouses decide how to spend their money on what they need and what they want. There is a difference. We *need* food, clothing, shelter, medical care, and many other things. But we also *want* things like a new car, a bigger home, more clothes, and better furniture. A budget helps put the needs and wants in perspective and can provide a way to work together toward purchasing some of the wants. It's surprising how many couples do not have a budget. If you do not have a budget, get help in developing one and stick to it.

The discussion on finances often becomes complicated by issues of control. A wife wants to control her husband's spending or a husband wants to control his wife's. On the one hand, perhaps control may be an issue because one spouse has demonstrated an inability to keep spending habits under control. On the other hand, the desire to control finances may be a symptom of a power struggle in the relationship. In that case, the couple needs to return to the concept of "one plus one equals one." The struggle for power and control over a spouse will show up in other areas too and will often cause continued friction until both partners can resolve it.

The discussion on finances often becomes complicated by issues of control.

Many marriages are torpedoed by the availability of easy credit. People can purchase large items with little or no money down and pay for them over a period of time. Credit is an important tool in handling the finances of a marriage as well as a large corporation, but whatever someone borrows must be paid back with interest. It is very easy for anyone to overextend and quickly pile up a large debt. Sadly, more than one marriage has slowly slipped underneath a sea of too much debt. Susan and Steven both spent excessively and created financial problems for themselves. Susan used the credit card; Steven bought a boat and a truck. In their case, the debt that resulted added tension to their already difficult relationship. Don't spend more money than you have coming in!

In contemporary society many marriages are two income marriages. Husbands and wives can find this a great advantage, but it can also add to the difficulty over money. Remember that whatever was "mine" before the marriage is best understood as "ours" after the marriage. Spouses are once again encouraged to use a budget; it will provide a way you can discuss your finances.

5. Unrealistic expectations of marriage

Sally married Jack. They both professed their love for each other and promised to live for each other. Shortly after the wedding, Sally sought counseling because Jack had a drinking problem. In the counseling session, she painfully shared the problem. When asked, "Didn't you know he had a problem with drinking while you were dating?" her response was, "Yes, but I thought I could change him once we were married."

Some couples may enter into their relationship with the notion that once they marry and settle into their little cottage with the white picket fence, marriage will be an ongoing experience of peace, harmony, tranquillity, and unending joy. Reality reveals that there is nothing magical about walking down the aisle. Marriage will never be perfect. There is no perfection on this side of heaven. Two human beings join together in marriage. Neither of them is perfect. Differences of opinions, attitudes, and background can create conflict. Problems will arise. But with God's grace they can build a happy marriage despite the imperfections in each other.

We can't change our spouses any more than we can change any other person. Change within any person takes place through the power of the Holy Spirit working through the

Word. You can change; I can change—but I can't change you, nor can you change me. In love we learn to live together.

We can't change our spouses any more than
we can change any other person.

6. Alcohol or other substance abuse

Scripture reminds us to "do all things in moderation." Alcohol or other drugs when misused will destroy a relationship. Substance abuse destroys the glue that holds relationships together. It undermines trust and destroys mutual respect. Because an individual becomes a slave to a habit or dependency, it frustrates the ability of the spouse with the problem to help the other spouse. Those dependent on alcohol or other drugs turn their attention from the partnership to their need for the substance.

Substance abuse destroys the glue
that holds relationships together.

Such abuse is not something abusers can correct by themselves. Often they promise to make amends, only to fail. The failure increases the guilt, often leading to more abuse in order to avoid the guilt, and then increasing the dependency and behavioral problems. If spouses suspect that substance abuse or dependency is a problem, they must seek help for themselves and gain new skills for dealing with the spouse who is abusing.

Overcoming denial is difficult for the person who is abusing. Denial also becomes a factor for the spouse and other family members of one who is dependent on alcohol or drugs. Those who love the abuser often make excuses, cover up the problem, or straighten out whatever problems the abuser creates. This is called enabling and will only perpetuate the problem. It is not love because it permits someone they care about to continue in their destructive behavior. The situation will not correct itself or go away in time. Professional help is needed both for the abuser and for the family of an abuser.

7. Sexual frustrations

God created us as men and women. He intended us to enjoy each other sexually in the context of the marriage relationship. A part of our promise to love unconditionally is to willingly submit to each other in meeting our sexual needs. God directs us here too. 1 Corinthians 7:4,5 reminds all husbands and wives, "The wife's body does not belong to her alone but also to her husband. In the same way, the husband's body does not belong to him alone but also to his wife. Do not deprive each other except by mutual consent and for a time, so that you may devote yourselves to prayer. Then come together again so that Satan will not tempt you because of your lack of self-control."

Refusing the sexual requests of a spouse as a means of getting even or making a point is certainly contrary to 1 Corinthians 7:4,5. It can be disastrous to any marriage. It is the wise and loving husband who understands how his wife needs preparation for the sexual union. Sexual intimacy can be fulfilling for both husband and wife. Tenderness and consideration can help develop a better sex life, as surely as they can build better relationships.

From time to time, sexual difficulties may put a strain on the relationship. Such intimate thoughts may be difficult for husbands and wives to talk about without help. In those situations, it is best to seek the help of a pastor, Christian counselor, or a doctor to address the issues. A healthy sexual relationship will help build a marriage. An unhealthy one will place stress on the marriage and spill over into conflict.

From time to time, sexual difficulties may put a strain on the relationship. Such intimate thoughts may be difficult for husbands and wives to talk about without help.

8. Sexual, physical, emotional, or verbal abuse

There is probably no greater destroyer of trust and respect in a marriage relationship than when either a husband or wife becomes sexually, physically, emotionally, or verbally abusive. Society often assigns abusive behavior predominantly to men, but women can also be verbally, emotionally, sexually, and even physically abusive. A look at the passage from 1 Corinthians 7 cited above shows a different spirit. A husband's body belongs to his wife; her body belongs to her husband. They care for each other in that relationship. Normally, no one would think of deliberately abusing his or her own body. It is unthinkable to inflict deliberate pain on oneself. God suggests that it is just as unthinkable for a husband or wife to abuse each other.

If spouses unconditionally love each other and their children, they will not jeopardize that love and trust by abusing each other or their children. If a husband or wife has a problem with anger or other issues which can lead to abusive behavior it will probably not correct itself. Professional help is needed. Spouses living in an abusive relationship may need to develop a plan to insure their safety and that of the children. The plan should include revealing the abuse to a pastor, counselor, and law enforcement officials.

God certainly does not sanction abuse within marriage. Spouses experiencing repeated abuse may need to find a safe place away from the abusive environment through separation. The separation should serve as a wake-up call to the abuser, but most importantly the abused spouse should find protection from the abuse. Separation can serve as a safe time when spouses can seek professional help so that they can work together in a context of change. The abuser must address the issues that prompt the abuse. As the abuser addresses these issues with the help of a counselor, he or she can provide the setting for change. Together the abuser and the abused spouse can work together in learning the skills to rebalance and reestablish the relationship. Separation should not serve as a prelude to divorce.

9. Disagreement on how children should be reared and disciplined

Scripture reminds parents, particularly fathers, to "train a child in the way he should go, and when he is old he will not turn from it" (Proverbs 22:6). God wants his lambs to be trained. That means that parents should lead their children in the way God wants them to go, not the way the child's sinful nature wants to go. That requires discipline. But it also requires a plan.

On the one hand, God does not want his lambs to be trained with unstructured permissiveness. Proverbs 13:24 warns, "He who spares the rod hates his son, but he who loves him is careful to discipline him." On the other hand, God does not want his lambs trained by harsh, oppressive discipline. Physical abuse of children is reprehensible to the world we live in and especially to Christians. God also says, "Fathers, do not exasperate your children; instead, bring them up in the training and instruction of the Lord" (Ephesians 6:4). Parents who love God, love each other, and love their children must work together to develop a plan based on God's biblical approach to discipline. His plan is simply train my lambs in love, love them unconditionally, and discipline them in love.

When both parents cannot agree and support each other in the disciplining of their children, children can become very adept at playing one parent against the other. It is important that both parents project a united front to their children, showing that both parents know God's plan, are committed to it, and diligently and consistently carry out his plan. The difficulty in achieving a unified plan increases when children from previous marriages are included in the family. Such blended families can be a wonderful opportunity to repair the mistakes of a previous marriage, but they will present special problems. Overcoming the problems will require love, consideration, and understanding.

When both parents cannot agree and support each other in the disciplining of their children, children can become very adept at playing one parent against the other.

Like every other item on this list, a consistent approach to discipline requires communication and understanding. Parents who do not have a plan for disciplining children and do not show a team approach in disciplining their children will experience ongoing conflicts between each other and their children. Additional stress will be placed on the marriage relationship and result in conflict.

10. Cutting the "apron strings"

When God brought Eve to Adam, he established the first marriage. There God tells us, "For this reason a man will leave his father and mother and be united to his wife, and they will become one flesh" (Genesis 2:24). Spouses must "leave home" physically and emotionally in order to cleave to each other. That does not mean that either spouse severs all ties with parents. Each spouse should continue to show love, concern, and respect for his parents. But, remember, the relationship between husband and wife is the primary relationship. The special bond between parent and child changes at the marriage of the child; it becomes secondary to the marriage bond.

Husbands and wives can have difficulty developing a healthy relationship with each other if they cannot alter the relationship with their parents. Parents, even when they are well intentioned, can become meddlesome and intimidating. If spouses do not "leave . . . father and mother and be united" to each other, they will undermine the marriage relationship.

The ideal love

When one of the spouses, in unconditional love, freely gives and the other spouse takes, but does not practice the same unconditional love, the ongoing friction can set the climate for frequent conflicts. When both spouses do not, in unconditional love, freely give to each other but always expect their needs to be met by the other spouse, marriage will be an ongoing struggle of one conflict after another. Such couples become very adept at making each other miserable.

When both husband and wife freely give of themselves to meet each other's needs, marriage can be the mutually nurturing and satisfying union of a man and woman that God intended it to be. Unconditional love freely gives 100 percent to the other spouse and expects nothing in return. A good example of that kind of love is found in 1 Corinthians 13, the love chapter:

> If I speak in the tongues of men and of angels, but have not love, I am only a resounding gong or a clanging cymbal. If I have the gift of prophecy and can fathom all mysteries and all knowledge, and if I have a faith that can move mountains, but have not love, I am nothing. If I give all I possess to the poor and surrender my body to the flames, but have not love, I gain nothing. Love is patient, love is kind. It does not envy, it does not boast, it is not proud. It is not rude, it is not self-seeking, it is not easily angered, it keeps no record of wrongs. Love does not delight in evil but rejoices with the truth. It always protects, always trusts, always hopes, always perseveres. Love never fails. But where there are prophecies, they will cease; where there are tongues, they will be stilled; where there is knowledge, it will pass away. For we know in part and we prophesy in part, but when perfection comes, the imperfect disappears. When I was a child, I talked like a child, I thought like a child, I reasoned like a child. When I became a man, I put childish ways behind me. Now we see but a poor reflection as in a mirror; then we shall see face to face. Now I know in part; then I shall know fully, even as I am fully known. And now these three remain: faith, hope and love. But the greatest of these is love.

If husbands and wives could practice what is written in that love chapter, there would be no reason to write this section or this book.

EXERCISES

1. Take a look again at the ten indicators. Identify as many indicators that apply to the marriage of Steven and Susan. Discuss with your spouse what Steven and Susan could have done to change their relationship.

2. Which of the indicators can you identify in your marriage relationship? Discuss your findings with your spouse.

3. After having identified the indicators in your marriage, list some things you can do to change, so that you can rebalance and reestablish your relationship with your spouse.

4. Begin to conduct devotions with your spouse and family. Start by reading the devotions printed in *Meditations* or another series of prepared devotions. Ask your pastor for suggestions on other appropriate devotions. You may feel awkward at first but keep at it. Remember that the gospel is God's power source.

CHAPTER 6

The Miracle of Forgiveness

Some of the hardest words ever uttered in any language are *I'm sorry*. A close second, if not a dead heat, in difficulty are the words *I forgive you*.

First, no one likes to admit being wrong. It goes against our very nature to admit we make mistakes. We would rather hide our failures. Whether monstrous mistakes or little white lies, it hurts one's pride to be caught in sin. It also hurts a person's self-esteem. To make a mistake and then have to apologize for it somehow leaves us all feeling weak, inferior, foolish, and feeble. Admitting a mistake also means that we lose authority, prestige, and influence. Satan loves nothing better than to convince us that confession of wrongs is a sign of weakness. And he does a good job in all of us.

Second, we find it difficult to say I forgive you and truly mean it. To forgive another person means we must let go of the wrong that was done. Our natural reaction is to hold on to the wrong because it gives power. When someone has wronged us, we can make use of that wrong to manipulate that person. Our sinful natures enjoy having someone come "crawling back on his knees." We love to bring up a past wrong, if only to assert our superiority. Sometimes we want to withhold forgiveness so that we can force someone to earn our forgiveness, to do something nice for us in order to prove he deserves to be forgiven.

At other times, saying I forgive you doesn't allow us to enjoy our own self-pity or to relish the moment of revenge when it comes. This chapter will hopefully show the joy of confession and the freedom of forgiveness. Through the miracle of forgiveness, we can see God work to restore what once was broken.

> After several sessions together with Pete, Janet came to the office alone for counseling. She just couldn't stomach the idea of sitting down with Pete in the pastor's office under the guise of seeking help. She wasn't sure she wanted help anymore. In fact, the first thing she blurted out revealed her spiritual crisis. "I just can't forgive him, Pastor. Not after everything he has done. Not after all the years of hurt and anger. He lied to me about his affair. I forgave him. He lied to me about his gambling. He lied to me about his long nights at work. I'll never believe another thing he says. And now I feel like he's desperate. He wants to put on a good show for you and demonstrate just how sorry he is . . . how much he wants to make it work. But I don't believe it anymore. I can't forgive him for all the times he has hurt me."

Her conversation revealed a crisis. Janet had come to a crossroads. Whether she knew it or not, several choices were beginning to focus before her. First, she could choose to hold a grudge and refuse to forgive Pete. Second, she could forgive Pete for his unfaithfulness and lies. But another set of options also were before her. She could reestablish the marriage with Pete or she could sue for divorce. Pete had been unfaithful and had already broken the marriage. In God's eyes, Pete's unfaithfulness had broken the marriage. Forgiving Pete did not mean that she had to reestablish the marriage. In addition, she had every reason to question the sincerity of Pete's sorrow. She could choose to allow him another opportunity to prove his faithfulness to her, or she could say that he had broken the marriage and she did not wish to renew it. But the first and most important crisis for Janet was over whether or not to forgive.

Achieving an attitude of forgiveness

When a person says I can't forgive, he really means I won't forgive. And when a Christian says I can't forgive, he is putting his faith into grave and serious danger. Consider what Jesus says in Matthew 6: "For if you forgive men when they sin against you, your heavenly Father will also forgive you. But if you do not forgive men their sins, your Father will not forgive your sins" (verses 14,15). Peter came to Jesus with the same feeling Janet had about Pete. He said, "Lord, how many times shall I forgive my brother when he sins against me? Up to seven times?" (Matthew 18:21). Peter's question asked if there was a limit on how many times he should forgive the same person for repeated sins against him. Jesus responded, "I tell you, not seven times, but seventy-seven times" (Matthew 18:22).

We will often find ourselves facing the crossroads of forgiving another or refusing to forgive. How can we be as free with forgiveness as Jesus suggests? How can we overcome the hurt, disappointment, and anger caused by another's sins so that we can forgive? There is only one answer. Jesus! In order to have the power to forgive others, we must understand the forgiveness Jesus offers to us. We have hurt him regularly with our sins. We have hurt him and disappointed him. Remember that our sins are responsible for the crown of thorns, the whipping, and the nails in his hands. Our sins are not one-time occurrences that do not happen ever again. No! We sin again and again. We are weak and fail often. Yet we have the boldness to come to him for forgiveness. Should he forgive us? No, he shouldn't. We don't deserve it. Does he forgive us? Absolutely, again and again. Each forgiveness gives us the power to strive to do better. Sometimes we succeed and do better; sometimes we fail. Yet he forgives us again and again.

There is only one answer. Jesus!
In order to have the power to forgive others,
we must understand the forgiveness Jesus offers to us.

As we are forgiven so freely by Jesus, we are to forgive others. By comparison with our sins against Jesus, the sins others commit against us are minor. We feel them deeply and hurt when others sin against us. Janet's pain was real and deep. But we have hurt Jesus more deeply and inflicted more pain, and he forgives. When we refuse to forgive, we reveal our own hardness of heart, our impenitence. For the Christian, forgiving another person is not an option. It is the fruit of a living and loving faith. As difficult as it was for Janet, she had to forgive Pete. That did not mean that she had to remain his wife, but forgiving Pete would allow her to release the pain, and it would give her the power to make the other choice—whether or not she could reestablish the marriage with Pete.

Jesus regularly emphasized the importance of forgiveness. After he answered Peter's question, Jesus told a parable about two servants, both with outstanding debts. One servant's debt to the king was staggering and unpayable. The king had compassion and canceled the debt. That servant went away free. Yet when that same servant ran into a fellow servant who owed him a relatively small amount, he would have no leniency or mercy. Instead of forgiving the small debt, he threw the man owing the small debt into prison until he paid up. When the report reached the king, he was furious. And so is God with that kind of attitude. Read about the parable in Matthew 18, and ponder what Jesus says at the end. "In anger his master turned him over to the jailers to be tortured, until he should pay back all he owed. This is how my heavenly Father will treat each of you unless you forgive your brother from your heart" (Matthew 18:34,35).

For those who have experienced the forgiving love of our Lord in Jesus Christ, forgiveness to others is a way of life. Yet Jesus knows it is difficult for our old sinful nature to forgive others, so he asks us to pray for the power to forgive. Every time we say the Lord's Prayer we ask, "Forgive us our sins as we forgive those who sin against us." We need other encouragements to forgive too, such as Paul's words: "Do not grieve the Holy Spirit of God, with whom you were sealed for the day of redemption. Get rid of all bitterness, rage and anger, brawling and slander, along with every form of malice. Be kind and compassionate to one another, forgiving each other, just as in Christ God forgave you" (Ephesians 4:30-32). Whether a person wronged us or not is not the issue. This side of heaven people will wrong us. We will wrong others. The issue is how we resolve those wrongs, both the ones we commit and those committed against us. Jesus says, "Forgive."

What is forgiveness?

Just exactly what is forgiveness? How would you put that concept into your own words? How would you explain it to your five-year-old? The Scriptures use concrete word pictures to define forgiveness and make it vivid. We can learn some important lessons from a brief word study on how *forgiveness* is used in the Bible. This study is by no means intended to be exhaustive. But the overview might help us picture in our minds what is meant by forgiving someone. Without going into detailed etymology or discussing every word, the following word pictures are helpful.

- One word uses the idea of "to cover." If a wrong is covered, it is no longer seen; it can no longer remind anyone of the hurt and offense it caused. The covering removes the offense from the mind's eye.
- Another word has the idea "to lift away, or lift up." A word related to that means "to send away, let go." Perhaps the mental image is someone or something moving away from us. We can imagine the wrong like an airplane leaving the runway. It moves farther and farther away from us until we cannot see it any longer. Finally we are unable to remember it.
- Still another word conveys the idea of "to cut away, to loose." Here I imagine a sharp knife or scissors cutting away the hurt and anger that tied someone up. Forgiveness cuts away the wrong committed against us and lets it go.
- A final word means "to be gracious." Who of us can't remember a kind grandparent who still smiled at us even when we had just run through the house with muddy shoes. We still got a hug. We still got the candy from the dish. Nothing we did destroyed that love and mercy from Grandma or Grandpa.

Forgiveness, as used in these examples, is more than just an abstract wish or verbal statement. It pictures a literal action; it demonstrates vivid results. How often do we take the time to picture in our mind's eye a sin being covered, so we no longer remember it? When we say I forgive you, do we imagine the hurt and wrong being sent away, as far as the east is from the west? We need to make forgiveness a concrete and vivid reality. If we don't, we have a difficult time releasing wrongs. Suddenly hurts and sins from decades back are still visible to haunt and hurt us. Wrongs from years ago still tie us up in anger and frustration. Just think how often arguments with a spouse spill all the old sins and mistakes kept in some corner of the heart. We are so good at remembering those insults, hurts, and lies. Let someone else make one mistake, and we'll never let them forget it. Forgiveness in such a situation never carries those sins away or puts them out of sight.

Wrongs from years ago still tie us up in anger and frustration.

Scripture uses the different word pictures for forgiveness only about 100 times. It might surprise you that the word *forgiveness* is not used more often in all those pages of Scripture. But you must realize that the Bible spends much more time explaining how forgiveness was established, first between God and humans, and then as a wonderful consequence, our ability to forgive other human beings.

How is forgiveness established?

We need forgiveness before God. Anyone reading this book would be quick to admit: "I confess that I am by nature sinful, and that I have disobeyed you in my thoughts, words, and actions. I have done what is evil and failed to do what is good. For this I deserve your punishment both now and in eternity" (*Christian Worship* page 26). What did God do to remove my wrongs from his sight? How did God send them away or cover them? How did God cut them loose? You have heard the answer often. Come back to Golgotha.

The cross is that "scissors" God used to cut all our sins away. No one is tied up in death and damnation any longer. If we use the picture of covering our sins, the blood of Jesus is that covering God used to blot our sins from his sight. This does not mean that God is some corrupt or lazy judge, who cares not a whit for justice. God is holy and just. Our sins were not just swept under some carpet and left there for us or someone else to trip over again and again. God is the just and righteous Judge; he has decreed that all sins had to be punished. If they had been left unpunished, God would be a liar because he plainly said, "Cursed is the man who does not uphold the words of this law by carrying them out" (Deuteronomy. 27:26).

God keeps his word. He cursed and damned all sin. But in love he placed that curse and damnation on someone other than us. He placed our sins on Jesus. "God made him who had no sin to be sin for us, so that in him we might become the righteousness of God" (2 Corinthians 5:21). At the cross, what do we hear Jesus say? "My God, my God, why have you forsaken me?" (Matthew 27:46). Jesus was forsaken by God because he was our substitute. He took our place and carried the curse we earned. So God tells us, "Christ redeemed us from the curse of the law by becoming a curse for us" (Galatians 3:13). God's justice was satisfied in his Son. Forgiveness is free to us, but it was not cheap. It cost Jesus everything! But, oh, the joy we experience when we hear Christ cry out, "It is finished" (John 19:30).

Does forgiveness mean forgetting? With God it does! Never will God bring up any of our past wrongs. Never does God replay a video of our sinful habits. Through the prophet, God says, "I will forgive their wickedness and will remember their sins no more" (Jeremiah 31:34). God is not blind; he sees all our sins. He is hurt by every failure. Yet God, who is all-knowing, lovingly covers our sins with the blood of his Son. He blots them from his memory. What freedom it brings. What joy to the heart! Of course, Satan keeps reminding us of all the lust, all the shameful deeds, all the horrible greed we have hidden deep within our hearts. Our consciences scream at times and Satan keeps reminding us of the heavy bags of guilt we carry. Satan whispers in our ears, "I don't think God can forget." But God is not like us. We can calm our screaming consciences with the forgiveness God has won by the death of his Son. God, in love and grace, forgives us in Christ. My sins and your sins are covered. God says, "I will remember their sins no more." What more glorious news can there be?

Does forgiveness mean forgetting? With God it does!
Never will God bring up any of our past wrongs.

Our forgiveness before God provides the basis of our forgiveness of one another. First it provides us with the power to forgive others. When we realize that God forgave us all we have ever done, we can forgive others. He moves our hearts to forgive by his free and undeserved forgiveness of us. Second, God's forgiveness is a model for us to follow. We learn how to forgive from God. He covers our sins so that he doesn't see them. He sends them away. He cuts them loose from us. He is kind and gracious in spite of our faults. All these things we can strive to do with the sins others commit against us.

God's forgiveness is a model for us to follow.
We learn how to forgive from God.

How is this forgiveness offered?

All people, whether they know it or not, crave such a precious gift. Without it we sense an emptiness and long for inner peace. An Old Testament prophet shared God's thoughts: "'There is no peace,' says the LORD, 'for the wicked'" (Isaiah 48:22). The nagging guilt of committed wrongs has driven some to despair and others to drink. Somehow and in some way, we want the hurt to go away. But we humans look in all the wrong places. We try to forget about the ache that gnaws at our spirits. We must keep busy, trying to ignore it. We try psychics and psychoanalysis, alcohol and chocolate. None of it works and if it seems to work, it doesn't work very long. It is only a virtual peace, much like virtual reality. When we take the images away, we find the familiar empty world of daily life.

God has established eternal peace between himself and all humanity through Christ. It is a reality the natural human heart wants to avoid and Satan wants us to doubt or forget. But our sins are forgiven completely. We do have eternal life in heaven because of Jesus. How can we know it, and how can we be reassured of it when doubts and problems plague us?

God offers real peace to us every time his glorious gospel is proclaimed in Word and sacrament. *Gospel* means "good news", and that is precisely the message God wants us to know. The Bible is full of the good news that all is right with God, thanks to Christ. Nowhere else can we find or experience the joy of forgiveness. That's why the psalm writer said, "I rejoiced with those who said to me, 'Let us go to the house of the LORD'" (Psalm 122:1). In the Lord's house, we find that rest for our souls. Through the gospel, the Holy Spirit creates a joy-filled and lasting peace. I am forgiven.

> *What makes worship and Bible reading so important is this peace that we can't find anywhere but in God's Word.*

What makes worship and Bible reading so important is this peace that we can't find anywhere but in God's Word. It will not float to us from the sky as we watch a beautiful sunset. We are not born with the knowledge of forgiveness and the peace it brings. The message of God's love comes to us as we hear, read, and remember the gospel and receive the Sacrament; and nowhere else. The message is so important because it is so unusual. Many religions speak of God's love and benevolence, but only true Christianity speaks about forgiveness of sins through Christ by God's grace through faith. Among the thousands of messages we hear every day, only the gospel of Jesus Christ brings peace to the heart.

> *The message of God's love comes to us as we hear, read, and remember the gospel and receive the Sacrament; and nowhere else.*

But this gospel is not just reserved for "church use." Each Christian has the privilege of using this precious word of peace. Since we believe in the forgiveness God gave us in Christ, we can share it with others. At home and in our marriage, God wants us to use the power of forgiveness with our spouses. God wants us to proclaim what Jesus accomplished on our behalf. God wants us to nourish and nurture one another. We have forgiveness with God. Therefore forgiveness with one another is also possible by God's powerful grace. So why is there so much pain? Why so much difficulty in learning how to forgive one another? It sounds too easy. It seems so simple. It truly is, in Jesus. But perhaps first we need to clear away all the barriers and obstacles we erect to dim the message of forgiveness.

What are some of the barriers to forgiveness?

The first barrier to forgiveness is **Satan**. His name means the adversary, the accuser. Satan howls in fury over the victory Christ won. Satan knows he cannot undo forgiveness. He knows he cannot overturn the cross. Jesus himself descended into hell and returned again to prove to us that Satan is powerless. But that doesn't keep Satan from trying to get us to doubt our forgiveness before God. How often don't we struggle with the idea that some sins are just too big for God to forgive? Satan will always be there, hounding us and accusing us. We all will go to our graves with Satan whispering, "God can't forgive you. You know what you've done. You know what you're really like." This barrier eats away at our joy and our confidence.

Another barrier is our own **refusal to admit our mistakes and sins.** Whenever a relationship breaks down, we simply feel that we are not at fault as much as the other person. Sometimes we hear ourselves say, "Sure, I'll take my share of the blame. But after all, it's not all my fault!" But God is not interested in finding out who is more guilty. Only insurance companies want to know that so they can assess liability. Before God, we are all guilty. "For all have sinned and fall short of the glory of God" (Romans 3:23). Before him, we are all born spiritually dead, corpses filled with the stench of sin. King David confessed, "Surely I was sinful at birth, sinful from the time my mother conceived me" (Psalm 51:5). All too often we do not want to admit our shortcomings and sins to God or to another human being. We would rather argue about the guilt of the other person, rather than confess our own failures.

That leads us to another barrier we often erect. We humans are not as merciful and gracious as God is. He forgives freely. **We want to get even**. When we can't get even right away, we remember. At times we wait for our opportunity to do unto others as they have done unto us. Revenge, it has been said, is sweet. In the marriage relationship, getting even is common. One form of revenge is a kind of "one-upmanship" that trades insults and put-downs to see if one can say something that will be just as harsh or harsher than the comment made by the other. The second comes from a long memory that keeps track of every mistake ever committed. In the heat of an argument, we are bound to recite the list. We use the list as a way of getting even for a new hurt or new failure. For some, every argument seems to resurrect the old behaviors and the old failures. Even having the last word is a kind of getting even.

And what does this do to the marriage? Perhaps an illustration is in order. In South America, cowboys are called *gauchos*. These gauchos, like our American cowboys, often must rope cattle or animals and bring them down for branding. North American cowboys use the lasso. The gauchos use the *bola,* a rope with two or three stones or iron balls attached to the ends. With a circular motion, the gaucho throws the bola at an animal's legs. The balls quickly whirl around and entangle the animal, bringing it to the ground. Just listen to arguments between spouses sometimes. Listen for all the verbal "bolas" that are thrown around. They are intended to bring the other spouse down, a kind of verbal vengeance. Instead of finding ways to heal and build up, we look for ways to hurt and bring down.

Another barrier is a **lack of love**, the free and undeserved love that the Bible calls grace. God loves us even though we don't deserve it. Christ proved that love. God wants us to imitate that love and share it with others. We don't love properly when we think that others must deserve our love and forgiveness. We withhold forgiveness because others do not deserve it. But that's not the point. In order to build a relationship, we must find starting points to overcome the failures. True love is one of those starting points. It allows us to forgive, whether or not someone else deserves it. That undeserved forgiveness can be a starting point for the offending party to do better. Forgiveness turns the page so that better things can be written on the next page. When we withhold forgiveness because we believe the other person hasn't loved us enough or endured the silent treatment long enough, we fail to turn the page and start again.

In order to build a relationship, we must find starting points to overcome the failures.

Just how many walls and barriers have we erected in our marriages? For some couples, those married for several decades, the walls are sometimes high and the barriers thick. Hurts pile on top of hurt and are cemented solid with anger and frustration. After a while it even feels safer to stay behind the barriers, because then we might not get hurt so much anymore. It is scary to try to take the barriers down. It is scary because we know that most of the blocks in the wall are our own sins and our own unforgiving attitudes. The forgiveness of Christ allows us to let go of all our own failures and sins. Forgiven, we can start each day with a clean page. When we forgive each other, our relationships can start afresh each day. Forgiveness turns the dirty and smudged page of the previous day, week, month, or year out of sight so we can begin again.

Steps to the healing power of forgiveness

It's time to let God work the miracle of his forgiveness through Jesus. The exercise below is not anything profound or difficult. Rather, it is one way for spouses to teach each other about sin and forgiveness, and for parents to teach their children the same lessons. It is a simple step-by-step process of using the law of God to point out and confess sin, and the gospel of God to cut loose that sin and bury it in the tomb of Christ.

Spouses begin by taking a sheet of paper and listing their sins in the marriage. If we don't think there is much to write down, then we need to remember this passage: "If we claim to be without sin, we deceive ourselves and the truth is not in us. . . . If we claim we have not sinned, we make him out to be a liar and his word has no place in our lives" (1 John 1:8,10). In all honesty, we all could fill a notebook with wrongs that we have committed against our spouses. For now, each begins by listing just ten sins committed in the marriage. They should be specific and to the point. After spouses have written their lists, they can ask for the Holy Spirit's blessing with this prayer:

> *Lord Jesus, pour out the Holy Spirit on us as we talk about the sins we have committed against each other. These sins leave scars that hurt, and they will not heal without your love and grace. Enable us to confess our sins honestly to you and to each other, and then find the peace of forgiveness you achieved on the cross. As we trust your forgiveness, help us forgive each other freely today. Amen.*

Step 1 The husband begins with the first sin he listed. He confesses this sin first to God by speaking it out loud. He may wish to use this form, "Lord, I have sinned against you because I have not treated the wife you gave me with the love and respect she deserves. I have _____ (Example: lied to her). I am sorry for the pain I have caused, and I ask for your forgiveness because Jesus died for my sins. Amen.

Step 2 The husband then turns to his wife and confesses, out loud, this same sin to her for he has also sinned against her. As he confesses this sin, he should be specific and sincere.

Step 3 The wife first speaks the good news of forgiveness that God announces to all of us through his Word. Like Nathan of old, she can say, "The Lord has taken away your sin" (2 Samuel 12:13). Or she might say, "Jesus has forgiven you for he said, 'It is finished.'" Many other wonderful passages announce forgiveness and bring joy to the heart of a penitent sinner. Here are two more examples: "The blood of Jesus, his Son, purifies us from all sin" (1 John 1:7). "Blessed is he whose transgressions are forgiven, whose sins are covered" (Psalm 32:1).

Step 4 The wife now speaks her personal message of forgiveness to her husband. She may say, "The Lord Jesus has forgiven you. I forgive you. I place your sin of lying (or whatever her husband confessed) into the tomb of my Savior. It is gone, covered by his blood. I now cut it away from you and from me."

Step 5 The husband now prays and asks God for the power to change. Forgiveness always involves a change of heart and habits. John the Baptist once said, "Produce fruit in keeping with repentance" (Matthew 3:8). Paul says, "Therefore, if anyone is in Christ, he is a new creation; the old has gone, the new has come!" (2 Corinthians 5:17). The husband now turns to the one who has the power to grant him new life and new love toward his wife. Following this example, he might pray, "Dear Jesus, I ask you to help me. (If he confessed lying to his wife: Remove the lying tongue from me. Help me always speak the truth in love to my wife.) Keep me from the old habits of sin and grant me ways to show my love to her. Amen." This prayer can be said with confidence for Christ himself promises, "I tell you the truth, my Father will give you whatever you ask in my name" (John 16:23). God does not lie. He will indeed help us live to his glory and will strengthen us to be able to do it through the gospel.

Step 6 Now reverse roles. The wife should now confess what she has written on her list; the husband should offer forgiveness.

This is only one way for married couples to use the forgiveness of sins. There are other ways. Find a way that is comfortable for you. Adapt. One form that couples might wish to adapt for their use is "Private Confession" (*Christian Worship* page 154). Remember, the motivation for this exercise is not to "do it right" to get forgiveness. Christ has already won forgiveness for us. It is ours. Use the exercise to remind yourselves of what we have in Jesus, and what we can offer each other.

Conclusion

Satan, the father of lies and deceit, would have you close the book right now. He wants us all to say, "It won't work. I'll never be able to confess anything out loud. I won't be able to get my spouse to do this." Satan desires to convince us that our problems are beyond hope. But the Lord God has revealed his will for us and for our marriages in his Word. Through it he gives the power to heal, correct, and change. He offers the power to make marriage work. Before we think that forgiveness is impossible, remember that God works through his Word. The Christian couple has a powerful and life-changing advantage over every other couple. God has entrusted his Word of Life to them. The gospel message of forgiveness in Jesus does indeed bring peace, and it does bring changes.

This is not to say that we won't have hurdles to overcome. Sin brings hurt, distrust, anger, and despair. Looking back over all the years, some spouses can identify many hurts and note many emotional scars. But the process described above will not pick the scars open again. Nor will it pour alcohol over those wounds so that they might sting again. Rather, the forgiveness we have in Jesus is the balm that will heal the wound once and for all.

> *Sin brings hurt, distrust, anger, and despair . . .*
> *the forgiveness we have in Jesus is the balm*
> *that will heal the wound once and for all.*

Consider, for example, the scar you might have from surgery years ago. Let's say that you had your appendix removed. The incision scar is still there. Yet you can touch it, rub it, and it does not hurt. At the time of the surgery, there was much pain. But through the pain of surgery, God used the doctors to remove something dangerous and life-threatening. It took some time to heal. But now when you see the scar, you no longer think of the pain. You remember with gratitude how your Lord God sustained you and healed you. The scar is but a visible reminder of God keeping his promises to you. Think of emotional hurts and scars in a similar way.

Right now you very well might be in tremendous pain in your marriage. Yet God, the same God who can heal the body, can also heal the soul and heal the relationship. Through the forgiving power of Jesus' love, the hurt can heal. Someday you can even talk about the emotional scar. Point to it with wonder at God's power to heal and change. More than once, pastors have seen the miracle of forgiveness work through the power of Christ Jesus. Yes, couples have returned years later and rejoiced that God healed their relationships. The scars of adultery, abuse, or alcoholism were no longer painful. What remained was a powerful reminder that with God, nothing is impossible.

EXERCISES

1. Review the steps of healing outlined in the chapter. Use your own words to describe each step.

    Step 1

    Step 2

    Step 3

    Step 4

    Step 5

    Step 6

2. One of the great difficulties you will face is learning to confess specific sins. It is quick and easy to say, "I'm sorry. I'm a sinner." One of the ways we avoid the harsh indictment of God's law is to generalize. Read the passage below and consider the specific ways the sinful nature has promoted sinful acts and attitudes.

    The acts of the sinful nature are obvious: sexual immorality, impurity and debauchery; idolatry and witchcraft; hatred, discord, jealousy, fits of rage, selfish ambition, dissensions, factions and envy; drunkenness, orgies, and the like. I warn you, as I did before, that those who live like this will not inherit the kingdom of God. (Galatians 5:19-21)

3. Sometimes we will also doubt the forgiveness of God. Confession is incomplete if it does not come with the assurance of forgiveness before God. The passages below bring us the assurance of God's forgiveness. Remember they are the promises of God. He stands behind his promises.

> Blessed is he whose transgressions are forgiven, whose sins are covered. Blessed is the man whose sin the LORD does not count against him and in whose spirit is no deceit.
>
> When I kept silent, my bones wasted away through my groaning all day long. For day and night your hand was heavy upon me; my strength was sapped as in the heat of summer.
>
> Then I acknowledged my sin to you and did not cover up my iniquity. I said, "I will confess my transgressions to the LORD"— and you forgave the guilt of my sin. (Psalm 32:1-5)

> Out of the depths I cry to you, O LORD; O Lord, hear my voice. Let your ears be attentive to my cry for mercy. If you, O LORD, kept a record of sins, O Lord, who could stand? But with you there is forgiveness; therefore you are feared. (Psalm 130:1-4)

4. The forgiveness of sins helps renew our desire to change and live as God wants us to live. But our Christian life needs some direction from God and some specific resolve from us as believers under the Holy Spirit's influence. Read the passage below and write down how you can change your behavior so it conforms more to the pattern God reveals.

> So I say, live by the Spirit, and you will not gratify the desires of the sinful nature. For the sinful nature desires what is contrary to the Spirit, and the Spirit what is contrary to the sinful nature. They are in conflict with each other, so that you do not do what you want. But if you are led by the Spirit, you are not under law. . . . But the fruit of the Spirit is love, joy, peace, patience, kindness, goodness, faithfulness, gentleness and self-control. Against such things there is no law. Those who belong to Christ Jesus have crucified the sinful nature with its passions and desires. Since we live by the Spirit, let us keep in step with the Spirit. (Galatians 5:16-18,22-25)

Epilogue

In one word, what does your marriage need? You might answer "love." And that is correct. But remember to use the Bible's definition of love. God's love gave without considering what it would receive in return. Love that heals, nurtures, and forgives is the love that comes only from Jesus Christ. It is vital to remember how God wants to teach you about loving. Slowly read God's definition of love and loving.

Dear friends, let us love one another, for love comes from God. Everyone who loves has been born of God and knows God. Whoever does not love does not know God, because God is love. This is how God showed his love among us: He sent his one and only Son into the world that we might live through him. This is love: not that we loved God, but that he loved us and sent his Son as an atoning sacrifice for our sins. Dear friends, since God so loved us, we also ought to love one another. No one has ever seen God; but if we love one another, God lives in us and his love is made complete in us.

We know that we live in him and he in us, because he has given us of his Spirit. And we have seen and testify that the Father has sent his Son to be the Savior of the world. If anyone acknowledges that Jesus is the Son of God, God lives in him and he in God. And so we know and rely on the love God has for us.

God is love. Whoever lives in love lives in God, and God in him. In this way, love is made complete among us so that we will have confidence on the day of judgment, because in this world we are like him. There is no fear in love. But perfect love drives out fear, because fear has to do with punishment. The one who fears is not made perfect in love.

We love because he first loved us. If anyone says, "I love God," yet hates his brother, he is a liar. For anyone who does not love his brother, whom he has seen, cannot love God, whom he has not seen. And he has given us this command: Whoever loves God must also love his brother. (1 John 4:7-21)

May the Holy Spirit of God fill you with that forgiving and giving love that comes only from Christ. Then, by his grace and power, you will be a sermon on true and lasting love to your spouse, to your children, and to all who know you.

Exercises

1. Christians desire to fulfill God's pattern of love. Spouses are especially interested in love. Using the words of 1 Corinthians 13, insert your own name below where the word *love* or *it* (referring to love) appears in the passage.

   _____ is patient. _____ is kind. _____ does not envy. _____ does not boast, is not proud, is not rude, is not self-seeking. _____ is not easily angered. _____ keeps no record of wrongs. _____ does not delight in evil but rejoices with the truth. _____ always protects, always trusts, always hopes, always perseveres.

2. Take hold of your spouse's hand and together pray either the following prayer or another prayer:

   Dear heavenly Father, you have bound us together as husband and wife. We have often hurt one another because we have been thoughtless and careless. Forgive us of the sins we have inflicted upon each other. We desire to live in peace and to deepen our love; help us overcome our own weaknesses and faults so that we might love each other as you have loved us. We come to you as your dear children in the name of Jesus, our Savior, asking for your power and help. Amen.

3. Recognize that the power to live according to God's plan for husband and wife comes from the gospel in his Word and the Sacrament of the Altar. Worship together. Conduct regular devotions together. Attend the Lord's Supper together.

4. Make a date with your spouse. Choose a special restaurant, make a reservation, and enjoy the special occasion. Other options include a concert or picnic. Whatever you choose, make it special, and make it an event for just the two of you to enjoy.

Marriage Inventory

Take a few minutes to evaluate where you are in your marriage now compared to where, with God's help, you could be.

Study each of the ten areas that follow; notice that number ten has two parts. This is an alternative for couples who do not have children or are not presently parenting children. Both husband and wife are encouraged to take a sheet of paper and, using the ten areas of the marriage relationship, take the inventory separately.

Evaluate your marriage on a scale of one to ten. The higher the number, the more positive you feel about that area of your marriage. The lower the number, the more improvement you feel is needed in that area.

When you have completed the inventory, add up your numbers and subtract the total from 100. If your total is 100, you believe your marriage is perfect in all areas. Of course, most marriages are not perfect. Your score will reveal how much your relationship can grow. For example, if your total is 45, subtracting it from 100 shows that you have 55 percent room for growth.

Compare your percentages. If your percentages are very close, it may mean you are in close agreement about your marriage. If, however, there is a significant difference in your percentages, it indicates that you and your spouse should discuss your differing perceptions of your relationship. This can be difficult. You must listen carefully to what your spouse is saying and not react to what you think is an accusation.

Next, go over your individual ratings for each of the ten areas. Again, significant differences should be discussed. Low ratings should not be viewed as negative but as opportunities for improvement and growth.

Finally, after having discussed the inventory, you and your spouse are encouraged to commit to a plan for change. This could include rereading this book, spending more time together, or seeing your pastor or a Christian counselor. Some spouses need an outside counselor to assist in acquiring the skills to rebalance and reestablish the marriage relationship.

_____	1. We share and show our spiritual life together.
_____	2. We are committed to growing in our marriage.
_____	3. We share common goals and values.
_____	4. We communicate in a positive way.
_____	5. We can resolve conflicts in a healthy way.
_____	6. We have a healthy sexual relationship.
_____	7. We manage our finances in a cooperative, responsible way.
_____	8. We have a good understanding of our roles as husband and wife.
_____	9. We show our appreciation for each other through mutual respect and concern.
_____	10a. We work as a team in parenting the children.
_____	10b. We consult with each other regarding major decisions.

_____ **Total**

Adapted from Henry and Vera Mace, *How to Have a Happy Marriage,* (Nashville: Arlington Press, 1985), p. 53.

Notes

Chapter 1

[1]R. C. Reins, *Treasury of Themes and Illustrations*, (Milwaukee: Northwestern Publishing House, 1983), p. 251.

[2]"The Worldling and the Believers Look at Marriage," *What Luther Says: An Anthology*, Vol. 2, compiled by Ewald M. Plass, (St. Louis: Concordia Publishing House, 1959), p. 885.

Chapter 3

[1]Cecil Osborne, *The Art of Understanding Your Mate*, (Grand Rapids, Michigan: Zondervan Publishing House, 1970), p. 52.

[2]Gary Smalley, *The Joy of Committed Love* (Grand Rapids, Michigan: Zondervan Publishing House,.1984, Revised 1988), p. 14.

[3]Smalley, p. 197.

[4]James Dobson, *Dr. Dobson Answers Your Questions About Marriage and Sexuality*, (Wheaton, Illinois: Tyndale House Publishers, 1982), p. 67.

[5]Paul Popenoe, "Are Women Really Different?" *Family Life*, Vol. 13 (February, 1971).

[6]Smalley, p. 196.

Additional Resources

Gary Smalley and John Trent, *The Language of Love*, (Pomona, California: Focus on the Family Publishing, 1988).

Richard Restock, *The Brain* (New York: Bantam Books, 1984), pp. 242-245.

Robert Gay, *Sexual Differentiation of the Brain*, (Cambridge: MIT Press).

Pierre Flor-Henry, "On Certain Aspects of the Localization of the Cerebral Systems Regulating and Determining Emotion," *Biological Psychiatry*, Vol. 14 (1985), pp. 4-14.

J. B. Hutchinson, *Biological Determinants of Sexual Behavior*, (New York: John Wiley and Sons, 1978).